PREPARING FOR MARRIAGE

God's Way

DR. WAYNE MACK

About Photocopying This Book

Some people who would never walk into a store and shoplift a book may think nothing of photocopying the same book. The results are the same. Both acts are wrong. Many people have the mistaken understanding that making copies of copyrighted material is legal if it is for their own personal use and not for resale. Making unauthorized copies of any copyrighted material is against Federal law for any purpose and may result in imprisonment and fines up to $50,000.

I Timothy 5:17,18 instructs us to give the laborer his wages, specifically those who labor in the Word and doctrine. As the publisher we have a moral as well as a legal responsibility to see that our authors receive fair compensation for their efforts. Many of them depend on the income from the sale of these books as their sole livelihood. So, for that matter, do the artists, printers, and the numerous other people who work to make these books available to you.

Please help us abide by the laws of both man and God by discouraging those who would copy this material in lieu of purchase. Since this book is protected by USA copyright laws and treaties, we would appreciate being notified of any violations.

HENSLEY
PUBLISHING

ISBN 1-56322-019-9

FOREWORD

As indicated by the title of this study, this manual is designed to help you prepare for a God-honoring and personally satisfying relationship in marriage.

Primarily, it was developed to provide you a carefully outlined, Biblical, thorough and practical tool for assisting you to be as ready for marriage as you possibly can.

It has been said that "an ounce of prevention is worth a pound of cure" and that "those who act in haste often sorrow in leisure." It is our sincere prayer and hope that the proper use of this study guide will be a means God uses to diminish the need for the pound of cure and the sorrow and disappointment which often occur when men and women enter into marriage without adequate preparation.

You may use this manual in one of four ways:

1. If you are seriously considering marriage, you will definitely profit by using it as a basis for a self-directed premarital study course. In this case, you and your proposed mate should work the assignments in each of your manuals, then get together to discuss your notes and your answers.

2. A second way to use the manual is with a marriage counselor. In this case, the study manual would actually provide the basis for the counseling sessions. You and your counselor would prepare for each session by studying the material in the manual.

3. You could also use this manual as a study guide in group sessions. A number of couples seriously considering marriage could make up a special class for this purpose.

In a class setting, the leader could use the manual to teach from and as a format for generating lively discussions. This kind of preparation could be invaluable to you as a couple.

4. The fourth use is a combination of one and two. In this instance, you first work through each lesson on your own and turn in your exercises to your counselor, who would then decide how much individual counseling you need on the basis of your answers.

However you use this manual, it will help you immensely in assessing your marital readiness. It will aid you in uncovering problems that may already exist and will provide you Biblical solutions and guidelines for resolving them.

Preparing for Marriage God's Way will also give you topics for dealing with the inevitable difficulties that will arise after your wedding and encourage you to establish patterns of relating and communicating in order to resolve conflicts.

Indeed, taking this course of study seriously could be the launching pad for moving you into a marriage that is truly satisfying and fulfilling. It will certainly prepare you for marriage God's way.

Wayne A. Mack

PREFACE

Marriage, however glamorized in today's world, is still God's idea. He made the first man and woman. And He conducted the first wedding ceremony, after counseling Adam and Eve on His design for a happy marriage.

But something is wrong today when one out of two marriages ends in the divorce court. The sacred institution of marriage is obviously in deep trouble. PREPARING FOR MARRIAGE GOD'S WAY addresses that problem. It provides a structured, comprehensive, Bible-based program for building stronger, happier, permanent marriages.

Dr. Wayne Mack, minister, teacher, nationwide lecturer and counselor, has been dealing with the subject of marriage for 26 years. Out of his years of counseling couples came the idea for a practical, in-depth guide to preparing for a happy marriage according to God's principles. The result is PREPARING FOR MARRIAGE GOD'S WAY. Before ever reaching the publishing stage, this unique course was "road tested" with hundreds of couples and proven to produce stronger, happier, permanent marriages.

It does this by giving you seven basic tools for a successful marriage. It enables you to: (1) assess your marital readiness; (2) know the other person for what he/she really is; (3) uncover any current problems and pinpoint future ones; (4) understand the solutions for both current and future difficulties; (5) develop skills for communication and conflict resolution; (6) prevent future heartache, and (7) prepare for a satisfying, fulfilling and God-honoring marriage.

Moreover, PREPARING FOR MARRIAGE GOD'S WAY teaches you how to get along with in-laws, as well as the place of God, Christ, the Bible and the Church in your marriage. Also, you'll learn how to deal with anger and resentment and to handle problems with sex and money.

To help accomplish all this and make it easy and fun for you to learn, the authors have incorporated many exercises and assessment inventories, all of which will help you understand both your mate and your marriage better.

Is this course for you? Yes, if you are engaged to be married. Yes, if you're planning on being married someday. And if you are newly married? Yes, definitely.

Also, PREPARING FOR MARRIAGE GOD'S WAY is for individuals who do premarital counseling and who teach counseling. In fact, anyone involved in the relationship of marriage can benefit immensely from the course.

If you are among the first group, PREPARING FOR MARRIAGE GOD'S WAY will help you build your marriage on a foundation strong enough to protect you from the despair and discouragement which so often lead to divorce and sometimes disaster. It will help you know yourself, know your partner, and know God in a lasting and fulfilling way. And finally, it will bring joy and happiness to your marriage, along with a greater capacity to love and respect each other from this day forward.

CONTENTS

ABOUT THE AUTHOR

Dr. Wayne Mack is Chairman of the undergraduate and graduate Biblical Counseling Department at the Master's College and Seminary in Sun Valley, California. He is also Chairman of the Family Ministries Council at Grace Community Church in Sun Valley.

Dr. Mack is a graduate of Wheaton College (B.S.) and the Reformed Episcopal Seminary (M.Div.). He earned his doctorate from Westminster Theological Seminary with an emphasis in pastoral counseling.

He has taken extensive graduate studies at Wheaton Graduate School, Trinity Seminary, Eastern Baptist Theological Seminary and LaSalle University. Counseling and psychology has been his major emphasis at the graduate level.

In addition to over 16 years pastoral experience, Dr. Mack has over 35 years of experience in diverse aspects of individual, marital and family counseling and administrative experience in counseling centers. He has been instrumental in starting three counseling centers.

Dr. Mack has directed, taught, and practiced counseling at the Christian Counseling and Educational Foundation Lehigh Valley; Christian Counseling Center of Lake Charles, Louisiana; The Conservative Baptist Seminary of the East; Biblical Theological Seminary, and Westminster Theological Seminary.

He travels widely and is well known as a speaker. His extensive training in Bible studies, theology and counseling places him in constant demand. He teaches and lectures nationally and internationally and serves on the boards of several Christian organizations.

Dr. Mack has developed several correspondence courses in counseling and has written many books in addition to producing numerous audio and video tapes on subjects dealing with practical Christian living as well as marriage and family development.

He has served as assistant pastor, youth pastor, pastor, director of various counseling centers, supervisor of counselors, pastoral counselor, and professor of biblical counseling.

He and his wife Carol have been married for forty years. The Macks have four children and seven grandchildren.

Dedication

This book is dedicated to my four children and two daughters-in-law, who have been a source of great joy and encouragement to me: Wayne and Lynne, Nathan and Karen, and Beth and Joshua Mack.

Session 1:
CONGRATULATIONS!

Congratulations! to the two of you because you believe marriage might be in God's plan for your lives together. That is a wonderful thought and one which is certainly worth investigating.

Congratulations are also in order because you've made the wise choice of deciding to spend some time and effort getting ready for marriage. By this time, you may have talked to your pastor about getting married. If you have, he probably has already informed you that he wants to meet with you several times for premarital counseling. Possibly, if there are a number of couples at your stage in their relationship, he has recommended that you join a class designed to prepare people for marriage God's way.

Perhaps your first reaction to this was not all that enthusiastic. But whether enthusiastic or less than that, the fact is you're willing to make an effort to prepare for marriage more thoroughly. And that's great!

A lot of couples have never stopped to consider just how important it is to take time to make specific preparation for marriage. When they do, the vast majority of them agree that it makes sense to devote considerable attention to this matter. After all, getting married is one of the most important things you will ever do.

Your pastor/counselor/teacher will develop the rationale for this endeavor more thoroughly. Indeed, there are good reasons for working through a course of study designed to prepare you for marriage God's way. As you proceed, you will come to believe it to be one of the wisest things you've ever done.

In preparation for your first session, here's what you are to do. Each of you should carefully and prayerfully fill out the following evaluation questionnaires. After you've done these exercises individually, share your reflections with each other. Take all the exercises seriously. Make sure you do all the projects thoroughly.

After you're married, you'll be glad you devoted your attention to this endeavor. In fact, even before you are married, you'll see the wisdom of this careful preparation. For one thing, you'll get so much more out of, and be able to share more, in the *Preparing for Marriage* sessions.

More than that, if you're like many who have already completed this course, you'll see an improvement in the quality of your relationship even before marriage. So roll up your sleeves and get ready for a meaningful experience. Carefully do the projects prescribed for session one. Bring them with you to the session. Be prepared to share the insights you have recorded. And don't hesitate to ask relevant questions.

QUESTIONNAIRE NUMBER ONE: **Relationship History**

QUESTIONNAIRE NUMBER TWO: **Relationship Evaluation**

QUESTIONNAIRE NUMBER THREE: **Marriage Expectation**

Preparing for Marriage God's Way

1

RELATIONSHIP HISTORY

1. How long have you known your partner? _____

2. How did you come to know your partner? _____
   _____
   _____

3. List three of your best memories from your dating experience with your partner.
   1. _____
   2. _____
   3. _____

4. List three of your worst memories from your dating experience with your partner.
   1. _____
   2. _____
   3. _____

5. List several kinds of things the two of you like to do together.
   1. _____
   2. _____
   3. _____
   4. _____

6. What place should physical contact and physical involvement play in the relationship of people who are seriously considering marriage? What guidelines or standards should be allowed in this area? _____
   _____
   _____
   _____

7. What place does physical involvement play in your relationship? Do the two of you agree? Has this been a source of contention or disagreement? If the physical aspect of your relationship were removed, what would be left in your relationship? Is there any guilt or frustration that you have because of your physical involvement during your dating days? How have you maintained a proper balance in reference to expressions of physical affection? _____
   _____
   _____
   _____

8. What place should the Lord play in a couple's relationship? What place does He play in your relationship? How has and does the Lord make a difference? Do you talk about the Lord together? How do you make Him a vital part of your relationship? How have you worked together to make Him important? Can you honestly say that both of you are closer to being like Jesus because of your relationship with one another? How have you helped each other

spiritually? How have you hindered each other spiritually? _____

_____

_____

_____

9. What do your parents think about your getting married? What is their opinion of your partner? What do your partner's parents think about your getting married? What is their opinion of you? What kind of relationship do you have with them? _____

_____

_____

_____

10. Read the following article taken from Josh McDowell's book, *The Secret of Loving,* pages 97-98. (Article used with permission.) What should a person tell his intended about his past? His present? His sins? His eccentricities? His weaknesses? His struggles? His limitations? How much? What would be legitimate reasons for sharing? Are there legitimate reasons for not sharing? If so, what are they? After you have finished reading the article and answering these questions, are there any secrets that you should tell your partner? _____

_____

_____

_____

_____

"Chasing Skeletons" from *The Secret of Loving* by Josh McDowell, pages 97-98, Here's Life Publishers, Inc., San Francisco, CA. Used with permission.

A lot of couples come to me for counseling after they have become emotionally involved, and this one question that comes up again and again is, "How much of my past do I share with the person I love?" This issue causes tremendous agony for many. My advice is not to feel compelled to "tell all." If you know you are loved and accepted for who you are now, then your love is secure. However, if events in your past could cause either of you to question the relationship, you are on shaky ground.

A young man named Chris found himself struggling with this question. After listening to his story, I suggested he not share some of his apparent mistakes with his partner, *unless* his motive for silence was fear—fear that revealing his past would negatively effect the relationship and her love and acceptance of him. If this was his real reason for withholding the information, I would counsel him to share his past with her and to let her love be tested. If the fear was there, he would never feel able to open up to her completely, and it would continue to haunt him.

David Mace, in *Getting Ready for Marriage,* gives some

more insight into this area. "I offer you a simple rule about confessions. If you feel you must make them, and you are quite sure you can do so in a loving way that won't cause distress to your partner, go ahead. But if you are in doubt about it, follow this plan. Go first and make the confession in full to someone you respect and trust, and discuss whether it would be good to make the confession to the one you plan to marry. If the decision on which you both agree is not to do so, you should find that the matter won't worry you any further. You have shown your willingness to tell, and that is what matters most. If at some later time the facts should come out, and your marriage partner asks you why you didn't confess before, your reply is that you were quite willing to do so, and that you have in fact told someone (whom you could name). You then explain that you withheld the confession from your partner, because it seemed at the time to be the most loving thing to do."

Remember this, a clear conscience is like having a clean and properly prepared canvas surface upon which God is to paint the masterful painting He wishes your life to be. If the surface is dirty or the images left by a previous artist aren't blotted out, the painting will have great difficulty being all that is visualized in the mind of the Master Artist.

RELATIONSHIP EVALUATION

1. If you were asked to describe your relationship in one word, what would that word be? _____
_____

2. What word do you think your partner would use? _____
_____

3. What are some of the strong points of your relationship? _____
_____
_____

4. What are some of the weak points of your relationship? _____
_____
_____

5. What have you done to strengthen these weak points? _____
_____
_____
_____

6. In your opinion, what do you think are the most important factors that will make a marriage a success? (Be specific and thorough) _____
_____
_____
_____

7. What do you bring to the marriage that will help make it a success? _____
_____
_____
_____

8. What do you think your partner brings to the marriage that will help make it a success? __
_____
_____
_____

9. What can a couple do to prepare themselves for marriage? (Be specific and thorough). What have you done specifically to prepare yourself for Christian marriage? What else could or should you do? _____
_____
_____
_____
_____

MARRIAGE EXPECTATION

1. What thoughts does the word "marriage" bring to you? _____
_____
_____
_____
_____

2. What are Biblical reasons for marriage? Why do you want to get married? _____
_____
_____
_____
_____

3. What are some goals a couple might have for their marriage? What goals do you have for your marriage? What goals does your partner have for your marriage? _____
_____
_____
_____

4. What expectations should a person have for his or her mate in marriage? Why is it important to know specifically what each of you expects from marriage in general, and from each other in particular? What are your expectations for your partner in marriage? _____
_____
_____
_____

5. What expectations have you had for your partner? How has he/she fulfilled or not fulfilled them?
_____
_____
_____
_____

6. What expectations does your partner have for you in marriage? _____
_____
_____

7. What expectations has your partner had for you in your relationship? Which ones have you fulfilled or not fulfilled? _____
_____
_____
_____

Session 2:
GETTING TO KNOW YOU AND YOU

"**H**ello! May we have the privilege of introducing you and your partner to you." Perhaps when you read this sentence, you said, "How stupid can you get! I already am well acquainted with me and my partner.

Well, maybe you are, but since all of us are such complex beings, we can always get to know ourselves and others better. (The truth is the authors still have a lot to learn about themselves and their mates.) And so you have much to learn about yourself and your partner.

Knowing yourself and your partner in a deep and accurate way is important to the success of your relationship. Understanding yourself and the other person in an intimate and personal way is an essential requirement for developing and maintaining deep unity in your marriage relationship.

This session will help you explore and know yourself and your partner more fully. So roll up your sleeves, begin your effort with fervent prayer, put on your thinking cap, get your Bible, pick up your pen and go to work.

First, do all the projects by yourself. Write down what you learned about yourself and each other. Then get together with your partner and discuss your insights. Identify how you felt while you were doing the exercises, while you were discussing them, and now that you have shared the results.

Bring the completed questionnaires with you to your session. Be prepared to give your insights. Be ready to ask questions about anything that you did not fully understand and to raise any concerns that emerged from this assignment.

QUESTIONNAIRE NUMBER ONE: **Reasons for Marriage**

QUESTIONNAIRE NUMBER TWO: **Personal Character Inventory**

QUESTIONNAIRE NUMBER THREE: **Personality Inventory Chart**

QUESTIONNAIRE NUMBER FOUR: **The Desirable Husband and Wife**

QUESTIONNAIRE NUMBER FIVE: **Love's Language**

QUESTIONNAIRE NUMBER SIX: **How do you say I love you**

QUESTIONNAIRE NUMBER SEVEN: **Common Interests and Activities**

Preparing for Marriage
God's Way

REASONS FOR MARRIAGE

1. List ten reasons why you want to marry your partner.

   1. _____
   2. _____
   3. _____
   4. _____
   5. _____
   6. _____
   7. _____
   8. _____
   9. _____
   10. _____

2. How can you know that a certain person is the one for you to marry? What guidelines should be used? What led you to the decision to marry this person? How did you know that you should marry your partner? Why do you think you should marry this person? _____
   _____
   _____
   _____

3. How important is it for you to find the other person attractive or appealing? What attracts you or appeals to you about this person? _____
   _____
   _____
   _____
   _____
   _____
   _____

4. How does 2 Corinthians 6:14-18 relate to the issue of whom to marry? What does it mean to be unequally yoked? Does the person you desire to marry meet the directives given in this passage? _____
   _____
   _____
   _____
   _____

PERSONAL CHARACTER INVENTORY

On a scale of 0-5 rate yourself and your partner on the following qualities. The highest rating is 5 and 0 is the lowest. For example, if you are very patient, give yourself a 5. If you are not patient at all, give yourself a 0. If you are somewhere in between, rate that between 1 and 4. Circle any area where you and your partner rate more than 1 point difference. Discuss how differences or similarities might affect a marriage relationship.

Your Name _____ Partner's Name _____

QUALITIES	SCORE: You	Partner
1. PATIENT	_____	_____
2. ACCEPTING	_____	_____
3. STUBBORN	_____	_____
4. EASILY ANNOYED	_____	_____
5. RESENTFUL	_____	_____
6. FORGIVING	_____	_____
7. DOMINANT	_____	_____
8. SELF-CENTERED	_____	_____
9. GENTLE	_____	_____
10. PUSHY	_____	_____
11. A GOOD LISTENER	_____	_____
12. REASONABLE	_____	_____
13. CONSIDERATE, THOUGHTFUL	_____	_____
14. LONER	_____	_____
15. DEPRESSIVE	_____	_____
16. OPEN	_____	_____
17. EXPRESSIVE	_____	_____
18. PRACTICAL	_____	_____
19. EFFICIENT	_____	_____
20. NEAT, ORDERLY, ORGANIZED	_____	_____
21. EXTRAVAGANT	_____	_____
22. RELIABLE, DEPENDABLE	_____	_____
23. AFFECTIONATE	_____	_____
24. ATHLETIC	_____	_____
25. HANDSOME/BEAUTIFUL	_____	_____

26. PLEASANT VOICE   _____ _____

27. MUSICAL   _____ _____

28. GOOD DRESS SENSE   _____ _____

29. FORGETFUL   _____ _____

30. LAZY   _____ _____

PERSONALITY INVENTORY CHART

Study the following chart and rate yourself and your partner concerning your personalities. The words numbered 1 though 3 are to be used to rate yourselves. Use the letter "m" (me) to identify your propensities and the letter "p" to identify your partner's. For example, if you are usually outgoing, rate yourself 2 under the appropriate column on the left side of the page. If your partner is usually reserved, rate him/her a 2 under the appropriate column on the right side of the page. Each of you will have only one rating for each line.

	Slightly — 1	Usually — 2	Always — 3	Slightly — 1	Usually — 2	Always — 3	
FAST							SLOW
OUTGOING							RESERVED
BOLD							TIMID
CALM							EXCITABLE
EXPRESSIVE							UNEXPRESSIVE
OPTIMISTIC							PESSIMISTIC
FLEXIBLE							RIGID
ARTISTIC							NON-ARTISTIC
ATHLETIC							NON-ATHLETIC
LOUD							QUIET
LOGICAL							SENTIMENTAL
OUTDOORS							INDOORS
TRUSTING							CAUTIOUS
DETAILED							GENERALIZER
SPECIFIC							NON-SPECIFIC
PLANNER							DISORGANIZED
LONER							PEOPLE PERSON
OUTSPOKEN							RESERVED
CONFIDENT							INSECURE
GENEROUS							FRUGAL
SPENDER							SAVER
CONVENTIONAL							UNCONVENTIONAL
PRACTICAL							IMPRACTICAL
INITIATOR							FOLLOWER
RESPONSIBLE							IRRESPONSIBLE
PUNCTUAL							NON-PUNCTUAL
AGGRESSIVE							PASSIVE

Note where you are alike and different. Discuss with your partner ways in which the two of you are quite similar and quite different. Discuss how your similarities and differences have affected your relationship. Discuss what you can do to eliminate any negative effects.

THE DESIRABLE HUSBAND AND WIFE
(Based on Galatians 5:22,23; 1 Peter 3:1-7; Proverbs 31:10-31)

Read each statement carefully and then ask yourself, "Is this true of me always (4), often (3), occasionally (2), seldom (1), or never (0)?" Reflect on the meaning of each of the statements. Then, put a circle around the number that honestly reflects what is true in your life. Don't overestimate or underestimate (Romans 12:3). Then, go over the sheet again and ask yourself, "Is this true of my partner always (4), often (3), occasionally (2), seldom (1), or never (0)?" Put a circle around the number that honestly reflects your evaluation of your partner's life. Compare how the two of you are alike and different, your relative strengths and weaknesses. Think about and discuss the implications of your ratings for your marriage.

	YOU	PARTNER
1. I am fully devoted to God; I have a deep and meaningful relationship with God.	43210	43210
2. I am loving.	43210	43210
3. I am joyful.	43210	43210
4. I am peaceful.	43210	43210
5. I am longsuffering.	43210	43210
6. I am gentle.	43210	43210
7. I am generous, willing to share.	43210	43210
8. I am kind.	43210	43210
9. I am faithful, trustworthy, dependable.	43210	43210
10. I am self-controlled, disciplined.	43210	43210
11. I am noble in character.	43210	43210
12. I am respected and valued by my family.	43210	43210
13. I am devoted and loyal to my family.	43210	43210
14. My family can depend on me.	43210	43210
15. I fulfill God-given family responsibilities.	43210	43210
16. I receive praise from my family and others.	43210	43210
17. I build up my family; I am an encourager.	43210	43210
18. I am devoted to ministering to others.	43210	43210
19. I am consistent and steadfast in doing right.	43210	43210
20. I am an industrious, hard worker.	43210	43210
21. I am unselfish.	43210	43210
22. I am more concerned about internal beauty than external beauty.	43210	43210
23. I take care of myself physically; I am concerned about my appearance; but not excessively so.	43210	43210
24. I am able to enjoy life; I am not a workaholic; I am not overly intense or serious; I am a fun person to be with.	43210	43210
25. I am contented and satisfied; I desire growth, progress, Biblical change but am not overbearing about it.	43210	43210
26. I am courageous and confident.	43210	43210

27. I am considerate of others, putting them at ease, communicating respect and concern for them.   4 3 2 1 0   4 3 2 1 0

28. My speech is constructive and wholesome.   4 3 2 1 0   4 3 2 1 0

29. I seek to grow in wisdom, to sharpen myself intellectually.   4 3 2 1 0   4 3 2 1 0

30. I exercise foresight; I plan ahead.   4 3 2 1 0   4 3 2 1 0

31. I handle money wisely; I practice good stewardship.   4 3 2 1 0   4 3 2 1 0

LOVE'S LANGUAGE

(Adapted from *How Do You Say I Love You?*, Judson Swihart, IVP)

Rate yourself and your partner on the following ways in which each of you desires to have love shown to you. Use a scale of 1-8, with 1 being the most important and 7 or 8 being the least important.

If, in your case, the most important way in which you want to have love shown to you is by having the other person touch you, caress you, cuddle you, kiss you, that would be number 1. You would then put the number 1 in the "Me" column beside the number 4 statement. If in your partner's case, you think (do this without asking) helping is the most important factor, then that would be number 1. You would write the number 1 in the Partner column beside statement 1.

Continue rating the other items in order of importance. If, in your view, something that is not listed is very important, identify it on line 8 and give it the rating you think it deserves.

In answer to the completion questions that follow the rating exercise, write out your honest opinions. Think about why this project is important and how understanding these things could help your marriage. Consider also how a lack of understanding of these issues could affect a marriage.

	Me	Partner
1. Helping	_____	_____
2. Spending time together, being there, doing things together, being willing to communicate	_____	_____
3. Saying it with words, expressing appreciation and admiration	_____	_____
4. Touching, caressing, kissing, physical contact	_____	_____
5. Being concerned about opinions, feelings, interests, desires, likes, dislikes, listening, sharing, cooperative, solicitous	_____	_____
6. Being loyal, faithful, protective, trustworthy, supportive, unselfish, responsible, keeping confidences, fulfilling promises and commitments	_____	_____
7. Meeting material and physical needs, taking care of possessions, giving gifts, giving birthday or anniversary cards, trading places, doing fix-it jobs, etc.	_____	_____
8. Other _____	_____	_____

HOW DO YOU SAY "I LOVE YOU"

Complete each of the following sentences in one or more ways:

1. During childhood, I knew my parents loved me because they: _____
_____

2. When "down," I like my partner to: _____
_____

3. After an argument, I want my partner to: _____
_____

4. I gain a strong sense of inner comfort when my partner: _____
_____

5. I have strong affectionate feelings when my partner: _____
_____

6. I wish my partner would more frequently: _____
_____

7. If I wanted to feel loved, I would ask my partner to: _____
_____

8. The nicest gift I ever received from my partner was when: _____
_____

9. When I want to really show my love to my partner, I: _____
_____

10. The most meaningful thing a person could ever do for his/her partner is: _____
_____

11. I feel acceptance and worth when my partner: _____
_____

12. What I like best about myself is: _____
_____

13. What I like best about my partner is: _____
_____

14. What I like least about myself is: _____
_____

15. What I like least about my partner is: _____
_____

16. Two of the happiest things that have ever happened to me are: _____

_____

17. Two of the happiest things that have ever happened to my partner are: _____

_____

18. The hardest experience I have ever had is: _____

_____

19. The hardest experience my partner has ever had is: _____

_____

20. If I could do anything I wanted and knew that God would provide all the resources and guarantee success, I would: _____

_____

21. If my partner could do anything he/she wanted and knew that God would provide the resources and guarantee success, he/she would _____

_____

22. My greatest fear is: _____

_____

23. My partner's greatest fear is: _____

_____

24. Five things that I really enjoy doing are:
    (1) _____
    (2) _____
    (3) _____
    (4) _____
    (5) _____

25. Five things that my partner enjoys doing are:
    (1) _____
    (2) _____
    (3) _____
    (4) _____
    (5) _____

COMMON INTERESTS AND ACTIVITIES

How do you and your partner take part in the following activities? Check the appropriate space for each item. It is possible that neither of you does some of the activities. In those cases, you may get some ideas of activities to try together.

	Together	Both But Not Together	One Exclusively	One Primarily	Neither
Church (attendance and service)					
Reading					
Competitive sports (tennis, volleyball, etc.)					
Spectator sports					
Non-competitive sports (jogging, swimming, etc.)					
Outdoor activities (camping, walking, etc.)					
Social gatherings (family, friends, church, community, etc.)					
Clubs, organizations					
Art appreciation (listening to music, visiting museums, etc.)					
Creative and interpretive art (writing, painting)					
Hobbies (collecting, gardening, sewing, woodwork, etc.)					
Business and professional activity					
School functions or organizations					
Politics					
Motion pictures					
Devotions					
Shopping					
Table games					
Sightseeing (traveling)					
Entertaining friends					
Other _____					

Session 3:
REAL LOVE GOD'S STYLE

You're in love. Right? Well, that's great! Being in love is a wonderful experience. It's also a very crucial factor in a successful marriage. In fact, it's so important that if you don't really love each other your marriage will be a disaster.

When people fail to love or be loved, all sorts of horrible things may occur. Without love, life often becomes unbearable, personal problems become overwhelming, relationships deteriorate, marriages fall apart and families disintegrate.

Jesus certainly underscored the fundamental importance of love in His summary of what God desires of us. He said, "You shall **love** the Lord your God with all your heart, and with all your soul, and with all your mind. This is the first and great commandment. And, the second is like unto it, you shall **love** your neighbor as yourself. On these two commandments hang all the law and the prophets." (Matthew 22:37-39)

"What the world needs now is love, sweet love" is a phrase from a popular song. It's also a truth of life. Love is what the world needs—and love is what the two of you need if you are going to make your marriage a success!

Now, most people would wholeheartedly agree that to have a good marriage two people must love each other. However, at that point their agreement about love would often end.

Ask ten different people for a definition of "love" and you might get ten different answers. Or, what is perhaps even more tragic, you might get no answers. Very often those who talk most about love don't seem to have much of an idea of what love is.

People get married because they say they love each other. Unfortunately, many of them cannot define love, or they have an erroneous or inadequate understanding of what love is.

How can you know if you are in love without a correct understanding of what you claim to be experiencing? How can you know if you are loving or being loved if you don't know what real love is? The truth is, you can't.

And that's a serious problem in many relationships. That's why many people who think and say they're in love don't act very loving. That's why many marriages that begin with high expectations end in disaster. People thought they were in love, but they didn't know the essence of love.

So the question of what it means to really love someone is a significant question. It's one which you and every couple who aspires to marriage should seriously consider. It's a question to which you should have some definite, solid answers.

Some tell us that real love can't be explained. It can only be experienced. Now, this statement is both true and false. It's true in that real love, God's kind of love, goes beyond explanation. It's false in that God, who knows all things, has given us some very clear statements in the Bible about the nature and essence of love.

Preparing for Marriage
God's Way

Perhaps by this time, you're saying, "Come on, you've told us that love is important. We agree. You've stated that God does give definite information about what love is. What you haven't done is give us that information."

Well, thank you for raising that issue. That's precisely what this session is designed to accomplish. At this time, I want you to devote your attention to the crucial issue of what our infallible, all knowing, gracious God says about real love. Get ready to be exposed to and challenged by Real Love God's Style.

Complete the following worksheets. As you do, seek to answer two questions: 1.) What is love? 2.) How can I demonstrate my love to others?

Preparing for Marriage God's Way

TRUE LOVE

A. Look up the following passages of Scripture and write down what each of them indicates about true love. Note carefully what love isn't as well as what it is; what it doesn't do as well as what it does do. Note also the implicit as well as the explicit statements.

1. Proverbs 10:12 *(note carefully what love doesn't do as well as what it does do).* _____
_____
_____

2. Matthew 5:43-48: _____
_____
_____

3. Romans 13:8-10: _____
_____

4. Romans 14:14, 15: _____
_____
_____

5. Galatians 5:13-15: _____
_____

6. Ephesians 5:25: _____
_____

7. 1 Thessalonians 4:9, 10: _____
_____
_____

8. 1 Timothy 1:5: _____
_____

9. Titus 2: 3, 4: _____
_____

10. 1 John 3:16-18 (see also James 2: 15, 16): _____
_____
_____

B. 1 Corinthians 13 is the great love chapter of the Bible. No discussion of love would be complete without a study of this chapter. 1 Corinthians 13 describes God's kind of love, a kind of love which a Christian may have and express because of what God is doing and has done for him and in him. Study particularly verses 4-7, and write down the different elements of love. Beside each element explain what that element means in your own words. After trying to identify the meaning on your own, check a good commentary to get additional insights. Then, having written down the meaning of the phrase, recount at least one example from your relationship with your partner of how you can show this facet of love to your prospective mate.

Here are two examples:

1 Corinthians 13 statement: v.4—"love is longsuffering"

Meaning: Love is not impatient or nasty. Love is not fretful or intolerant. Love is patient, willing to suffer long without retaliating. Love gives the other person space. Love is willing to wait. Love doesn't manipulate or sinfully pressure the other person into changing.

Example: When my partner doesn't see things the way I see them, loving him or her means I will not try to coerce agreement with me by the loudness of my voice or by threats or by being critical, silent or by withdrawing. Love means that I will allow my partner to think differently. I will not attempt to overpower or force conforming to me.

1 Corinthians 13 statement: v.5—"love keeps no record of wrongs"

Meaning: Love forgives even when forgiveness is not requested. Love does not stew about the past. It chooses not to remember what lies behind. Love views each day as a new day and does not allow the past to ruin it. Love doesn't continue to review the ways my partner has offended me. Love keeps a record of the good things my partner does.

Examples: I will not hold a grudge or refuse to forgive my partner even when he or she repeatedly is late for our dates. I will not continue to think about the times when my partner forgets to do something I ask. Instead, I will think of the way he or she smiles when he or she sees me or, the way he or she prays for me or how he or she is helpful.

YOUR OWN WORK (you may want to even redo the samples by giving other examples that are more appropriate to your life and relationship. Write in the verse and then the statement as in the examples.)

1 Corinthians 13 statement: _____

Meaning: _____

_____

Examples: _____

_____

1 Corinthians 13 statement: _____

Meaning: _____

_____

Examples: _____

_____

1 Corinthians 13 statement: _____

Meaning: _____

_____

Examples: _____

_____

1 Corinthians 13 statement: _____

Meaning: _____

_____

Examples: _____

_____

1 Corinthians 13 statement: _____

Meaning: _____

_____

Examples: _____

_____

1 Corinthians 13 statement: _____

Meaning: _____

_____

Examples: _____

_____

1 Corinthians 13 statement: _____

Meaning: _____

_____

Examples: _____

_____

1 Corinthians 13 statement: _____

Meaning: _____

_____

Examples: _____

_____

1 Corinthians 13 statement: _____
Meaning: _____
_____

Examples: _____
_____
_____

1 Corinthians 13 statement: _____
Meaning: _____
_____

Examples: _____
_____
_____

1 Corinthians 13 statement: _____
Meaning: _____
_____

Examples: _____
1 Corinthians 13 statement: _____
Meaning: _____
_____

Examples: _____
_____
_____

1 Corinthians 13 statement: _____
Meaning: _____
_____

Examples: _____
_____
_____

C. Evaluate yourself as your partner's lover by using the criteria about real love that you have just defined and illustrated. Score Always true—4; Frequently true—3; Sometimes true—2; Seldom true—1; Never true—0.

1. I am longsuffering.   4 3 2 1 0
2. I am kind.   4 3 2 1 0
3. I am contented; I am happy when my partner has something that I don't.   4 3 2 1 0
4. I don't try to impress my partner with how great I am and how lucky he/she is
   to have me.   4 3 2 1 0

5. I understand that whatever gifts I have are by God's grace; I am not proud; I am not haughty or arrogant, thinking that I am superior to my partner; I consider his/her views and needs to be as important as mine.   4 3 2 1 0

6. I am not rude; I don't act unbecomingly; I am courteous and polite; I am considerate; I am mannerly and tactful.   4 3 2 1 0

7. I do not seek my own; I am not self-centered; I am not opportunistic or manipulative; I am willing to sacrifice; I am willing to change; I am genuinely concerned about my partner; I serve my partner.   4 3 2 1 0

8. I don't enjoy making fun of my partner or exposing his/her faults; I affirm and express appreciation to my partner; I am not critical; I bring out the best in my partner.   4 3 2 1 0

9. I am willing to forgive; I don't hold grudges; I don't keep a record of wrongs; I am willing to live in the present with my partner; I don't remind him/her of past mistakes.   4 3 2 1 0

10. I am loyal, faithful and trustworthy; I seek to protect my partner; I am willing to share and carry his/her burdens and problems; I keep confidences.   4 3 2 1 0

11. I recognize my own faults and the faults of my partner but still maintain a positive, hopeful attitude; I am not moody.   4 3 2 1 0

12. I am slow to anger; I am not easily annoyed or irritated with my partner; I control the expression of my anger; I don't attack my partner but seek to deal with the problem.   4 3 2 1 0

13. I am not suspicious; I trust my partner; I have confidence in her/him; I treat her/him with respect; I'm not constantly demanding assurance and reaffirmation.   4 3 2 1 0

14. I am committed to my partner; I will persevere in this relationship; I will be steadfast; I hang in there; I am consistent in acting toward my partner in a loving way; I realize that love is a choice I make and is not exclusively a matter of feelings or emotions; I choose to love even when I don't feel very loving.   4 3 2 1 0

D. Now that you have evaluated your love quotient, list all of the items that you scored 0-2. No one except Jesus Christ or the people who are already in heaven could score all 4's. Every one of us falls short of this standard, but it is the standard. God will not allow us to lower the standard just because we don't reach it.

After you have identified the facets of love in which you are most deficient, acknowledge your deficiencies to Christ and ask Him for forgiveness. But more than that, ask Him for His help in improving as real lovers. Christ is your Example and your Enabler. By His power, you can improve if you really want to. You can change if you are willing to recognize your failure, seek His power and specifically make plans about how you can improve.

Think about what you could do in practical ways to make sure you maintain and even develop more fully the facets of real love described in 1 Corinthians 13. Study the Bible to discover how love is developed and maintained. Write a brief article summarizing your discoveries. Be prepared to share your insights in the session. Be ready also to ask your counselor/teacher for his suggestions about improving as a lover.

1. List of love deficiencies: _____

_____

_____

_____

2. Plan for improving as a lover: _____
_____
_____
_____
_____

E. Make a list of the legitimate longings and desires of your partner. Think of his/her total life—
    physical, intellectual, spiritual, social, emotional, financial, recreational, etc. What does she/
    he need and/or want in these areas? We have seen that love involves helping other people, but
    you probably won't help unless you know where they need help. Don't sit around and wait for
    your partner to tell you. YOU have to be aggressive. Look for and plan ways to serve one
    another.

PHYSICAL NEEDS and/or WANTS: _____
_____
_____

What I can do to fulfill these needs or desires: _____
_____
_____
_____
_____

INTELLECTUAL NEEDS and/or WANTS: _____
_____
_____
_____

What I can do to fulfill these needs or desires: _____
_____
_____
_____
_____
_____

SPIRITUAL NEEDS and/or WANTS: _____
_____
_____
_____

What I can do to fulfill these needs or desires: _____
_____
_____

_____

_____

EMOTIONAL NEEDS and/or WANTS: _____

_____

_____

What I can do to fulfill these needs or desires: _____

_____

_____

_____

_____

SOCIAL NEEDS and/or WANTS: _____

_____

_____

_____

What I can do to fulfill these needs or desires: _____

_____

_____

_____

_____

FINANCIAL NEEDS and/or WANTS: _____

_____

_____

_____

What I can do to fulfill these needs or desires: _____

_____

_____

_____

_____

RECREATIONAL NEEDS and/or WANTS: _____

_____

_____

_____

What I can do to fulfill these needs or desires: _____

_____

_____

_____

_____

OTHER NEEDS and/or DESIRES: _____

_____

_____

What I can do to fulfill these needs or desires: _____

_____

_____

F. Write down what you are presently doing to serve your partner. Add to that list specific, tangible things that you might do.

1. Record how you are presently serving your partner. _____

_____

_____

_____

_____

_____

2. List other ways you may serve your partner and show love to him/her. _____

_____

_____

_____

_____

_____

_____

Session 4:
MARRIAGE, GOD'S STYLE

Marriage is a divine institution. It is God's idea. He made the first man and woman. He introduced them to each other. He gave them their pre-marital counseling. He performed the first wedding service. Without a doubt, He knows best what marriage should be and how married people should conduct their relationship.

Getting to know what marriage is, God's way, should be of great concern for every couple considering marriage. As two people sincerely and earnestly attempt to follow the blueprint He has outlined in His Word, they will find success and true happiness. The purpose for this session is to help the two of you learn together about God's plan for marriage.

An important concept to consider in preparing for marriage is the necessity of leaving your father and mother. You have already been directed to think seriously about this crucial part of God's plan for marriage. But you should go still further in exploring this issue by using the practical exercises found on the next few pages of *Preparing for Marriage God's Way.*

Each of you should carefully and prayerfully follow instructions and do the **Family Of Origin Study,** the **In-Law Relations Worksheet** and the **In-Law Inventories #1 & 2.** First do each of these studies individually. Then get together and discuss your individual ideas.

Another issue that you have already partially considered is the concept of cleaving or commitment. But again, you've only made a start in investigating this facet of God's plan for marriage. You must deepen your exploration of this aspect by completing the work prescribed on the **Commitment In Marriage Form.**

Preparing for Marriage
God's Way

FAMILIES OF ORIGIN STUDY

Discuss together the similarities and differences between your families. Write down your findings. Make sure you discuss the following items.

1. Family Occupations (blue-collar vs. white-collar, both parents work or just one, etc.)

2. Marriage of Parents (good, fair, bad, poor, still together, divorced, separated, etc.)

3. Family Rules (for example, "children should not argue with parents", "children do the dishes", etc.)

4. Personality features and characteristics of Mother and Father.

5. Family Beliefs (for example, "the family that prays together stays together", "cleanliness is next to godliness", etc.)

6. View about Finances (how money should be spent, saved, etc.)

7. Views about Sex (often discussed, never discussed, dirty subject, etc.)

8. Views about Responsibilities and Roles of the Husband/Father and Wife/Mother (for example, "mom always does the dishes", "mom always cleans the house", "dad mows the lawn", "dad makes the decisions", etc.)

9. Relationships with the Extended Families (grandparents, uncles, etc.)

10. Involvement in Church Activities, Spiritual things, etc.

11. Family Political Views

12. Views about Work, Recreation and Vacations

13. Family secrets (for example, Aunt Mary was pregnant when she married, Uncle John had a drinking problem, etc.)

14. Ways of handling problems, disagreements, ways of communicating.

15. Family values or standards.

16. Family boundaries: personal privacy issues, ideas about personal possessions, freedom to be an individual, liberty to have own interests, make own decisions, extent to which other people were allowed into family affairs, expressions of affection, attitudes toward fun, etc.

Answer these questions:
1. How are your families of origin alike and different?
2. How are your mothers and fathers alike and different?
3. What impact has your family background had on you positively and negatively? In what specific ways have you been affected?
4. How may your future marriage and marriage partner be affected either directly or indirectly?

IN-LAW RELATIONS WORKSHEET

1. Do you have any problems with your parents or your prospective in-laws? Write down the kinds of problems you have had. _____
_____
_____
_____
_____

2. What kinds of in-law problems have you observed in the marriages of others? _____
_____
_____
_____
_____

3. What are the most common mistakes that in-laws (children and parents, brothers-in-law, sisters-in-law, etc.) make? _____
_____
_____
_____
_____

4. Study Exodus 18, the description of Moses' relationship with his father-in-law, and write down everything you see about the kind of relationship that Jethro and Moses had. Try to discern why this was such a good relationship. _____
_____
_____
_____

   Turn to the Book of Ruth and do the same in reference to the relationship of Ruth and Naomi. What characteristics of Naomi should a mother-in-law model, and what characteristics of Ruth should a daughter-in-law model? _____
_____
_____
_____

5. Taking what you have just learned from the Bible, imagine that someone has come to you asking for your advice about how to develop a good relationship with his/her present or prospective in-laws. Write out what you would say. _____
_____
_____
_____

6. Identify what you could do to improve your relationship with your prospective in-laws. ___

_____

_____

_____

_____

7. Write a letter to your prospective in-laws expressing appreciation for them and indicating the kind of relationship you want to have with them. _____

_____

_____

_____

_____

8. Write a letter to your parents expressing your views on how you should relate to them, and they to you and your mate after marriage. A sample is included on the next page. Read this carefully and then develop a letter of your own. Bring your letter with you to the next session. ___

_____

_____

_____

_____

SAMPLE LETTER: CHILD TO PARENTS

Dear Mom and Dad,

I want to thank you for your love and devotion to me as I was growing up. You have been good parents, bringing me up in the counsel and the discipline of the Lord. You have been used of God to make me what I am. Through you, your words, your actions, reactions and attitudes, I have learned. To you I am deeply indebted and grateful and will always be.

At this time, a very important time in each of our lives, our relationship will change—not deteriorate but change, not disappear but be altered. Scriptures assert that for the cause of marriage shall a man leave his mother and father. Well, that time has arrived in my life. As a Christian I will always honor you, appreciate you, respect you, pray for you, commend you and seek to help you, but still God says I must leave. And in obedience to the God I love I will do that.

God says that next to my relationship to Him—or perhaps I should say as part of my relationship to Him—my relationship with my wife/husband must become the priority relationship in life. I am sure you will agree.

From the time of our wedding onward _____ and I will become one flesh. We want to have the relationship God intends and to be everything God wants us to be. I ask you to regard _____ as a part of the family in the same way as you regard me. After all, the Bible says we have become one flesh and he who loves his wife/husband, loves himself/herself. I ask you to help us to learn how to merge our two independent lives into a one-flesh relationship practically.

You have been given wisdom from God and from time to time, we will be turning to you for counsel. When we do, we will take your counsel seriously, but under God we will think, search the Scriptures and pray, and determine God's will for ourselves. We want, we need your continued love and assistance, but God has called us to establish a new family for Christ, developing our own unique lifestyle within the framework of Scriptures. We want to be your friends as well as your children. We want you to be free to agree or disagree with us and love us regardless. We want the same freedom. This will be hard for us and for you. After all, until this point under God you have been my Number 1 authority in life. I have come to depend upon you, to look first to you for counsel and support and assistance. Now that changes, and change is hard, for me and for you.

Please understand what I am saying—I/We want to be what God wants. I/We want our relationship with you to be a good one. I/We love you deeply, respect you greatly and are expecting that the future will bring new and enjoyable aspects to our relationship. Thanks again for all you are and have been to us. We love you.

Son/Daughter

IN-LAW INVENTORY #1

Rating Scale: 0 = not at all; 1 = some; 2 = very much

	You	Your partner
1. Excessive dependence upon parents	_____	_____
2. Jealous of partner's relationship with parents	_____	_____
3. Critical of partner's parents and/or relatives	_____	_____
4. Gossips to parents about partner	_____	_____
5. Critical of partner to parents	_____	_____
6. Takes sides with parents against partner	_____	_____
7. Excessive talking about parents	_____	_____
8. Compares partner to parents	_____	_____
9. Is partial to own parents	_____	
10. Puts parents above partner	_____	_____
11. Favorably compares own parents to partner's parents	_____	_____
12. Makes plans with parents without seeking partner's counsel/advice	_____	_____
13. Allows parents to dominate	_____	_____
14. Excessive desire to please parents	_____	_____

Now, summarize what impressed you about yourself and your partner in relationship to your parents.

IN-LAW INVENTORY #2

Rating Scale: 0 = not at all; 1 = some; 2 = very much

	Your parents	Your partner's parents
1. Fault finding	_____	_____
2. Meddle in our affairs	_____	_____
3. Have unrealistic expectations of our relationship	_____	_____
4. Are overly possessive and protective in our relationship	_____	_____
5. Are indifferent and aloof towards us	_____	_____
6. Are overly dependent upon child	_____	_____
7. Gossip about us	_____	_____
8. Insist on having their own way	_____	_____
9. Talk too much	_____	_____
10. Won't listen	_____	_____
11. Are unappreciative	_____	_____
12. Are jealous of other set of parents	_____	_____
13. Are jealous of our relationship with other people	_____	_____

Now, summarize what impressed you about your parents and prospective in-laws through this study.

COMMITMENT IN MARRIAGE STUDY

1. Read Psalm 15:4b; Numbers 30:2; Deuteronomy 23:21 and Ecclesiastes 5:4. What do these passages teach about making commitments?

2. In considering the following statement of commitment, (1) Write out the basic factors or principles that are included in it; (2) What would you include from this statement in your own marriage commitment? (3) What would you add to this statement? (4) What would you delete from it? How would you change it? Write your answers to these questions in the "notes" section.

Sample statement: "As I marry you, I am making a lifelong and irrevocable commitment to know and love God and to know and love you. I can learn to love you only as I come to know God's love for me. I therefore commit myself to daily seek to know God better by asking Him to teach me as I meditate on His Word.

I promise never to stop seeking to learn how to love you better. I want my love to duplicate the love described in 1 Corinthians 13. I want my love for you to be patient, kind and enduring, not jealous or envious; a love that is content with what God is pleased to give us; a love which is not proud or selfish, not rude or inconsiderate; a love that is gentle with your weaknesses and seeks to point you to Christ, not me; a love that responds graciously when we have a disagreement. Most of all, I want my love to be a love that points you to the source of all real love, our Savior Jesus Christ.

I commit myself to seek with God's certain help to love you with a love that overlooks annoying wrongs, failures, sins or inconsistencies, being glad to forgive and remembering that I have probably wronged and failed you more times than you have wronged or failed me; a love that remembers that I have wronged Jesus greatly and yet He died for me and forgave me; a love that is grieved when you are hurt or troubled or sinful and reaches out to give appropriate help, to restore and uplift rather than demean, despise, expose or condemn.

By God's grace, I resolve to love you with a love that does not demand its own way; a love that is creatively thoughtful and looks for ways to encourage; a love that is not self seeking, putting your needs before my own. I promise to protect you and stick with you. I will believe the best about you and seek to put the best interpretation on your actions and motives.

I pledge myself to a love that will know no limit to its trust, no fading of its hope; a love that will stand when all else around us has fallen. I covenant to give myself wholly to you and to pursue an exclusive intimacy with you. I dedicate myself to finding my ultimate contentment and satisfaction in Jesus Christ and not to seeking it from you or from any other source.

Preparing for Marriage
God's Way

I promise to share with you daily my thoughts, my dreams, my hopes, my joys, my successes, my troubles, my fears, my failures, all of my life. More than that, I will encourage you to share yourself with me—your thoughts, dreams, hopes, joys, successes, troubles, fears and failures, all of your life. And when you do, I will listen and care and share.

I pledge to give God the glory for anything good that He does through me. I marry you with the conviction that to be a good husband or wife, I must know, worship, and serve God first of all. I, therefore, make all of these commitments with the understanding that I must first of all be committed wholeheartedly to God; by His grace, that I am, and, by His grace, that I will continue to be. This is my commitment to God and to you.

Are you ready to make a commitment such as this? Yes _____; I'm not sure _____; No _____

Signed _____

3. And now having examined this sample commitment statement, build on the work you have just done. Write a statement describing your commitment to your partner by completing this statement: "I realize that the essence of marriage is commitment to God and to you. As I marry you, I commit myself. . ."

Make your statement personal and specific. Of course, you may use elements from the sample statement. But don't just copy it verbatim. Put your commitment in your own words. Make it a reflection of your understanding of what the Bible says about your responsibilities and privileges in marriage. Include your convictions about how you will fulfill and apply these principles in your relationship.

Preparing for Marriage God's Way

THE MOST IMPORTANT RELATIONSHIP IN YOUR RELATIONSHIP

For the past few weeks, you and your counselor/teacher have been discussing how to prepare for marriage God's way. You talked about your reasons for wanting to get married. You reflected on your similarities and differences. You considered God's plan for marriage and discussed the practical implications of that plan for your relationship.

In the weeks that lie ahead, you will be expanding your studies into still other important areas. In particular, you will be looking at the important subjects of communication in marriage, conflict resolution, husband and wife roles, finances and sex.

By this time you've become aware of the fact that good marriages don't just drop out of the sky on your wedding day. Successful marriages require work—and lots of it.

Good marriages are based on commitment. They are the fruit of a commitment to God and His plan for marriage. They are the by-product of a commitment to:

(1) the priority of the marriage relationship,
(2) developing a partnership and friendship in the marriage relationship,
(3) the permanence of the marriage relationship,
(4) expending whatever effort is necessary and Biblically legitimate to make the marriage successful,
(5) serve and help each other grow and develop into the person God wants each of you to be.

Face the fact that good marriages are not easy to develop or maintain. In good marriages people have problems, but they don't run away from them. Rather, they stay and work through those problems in a loving and gentle way.

Believe it or not, there may be times when you will not feel like loving your mate. Occasionally, you may not feel like serving. Now and then, you may not feel like working through problems. Sometimes, the thing you may feel like doing most is to tuck your tail under your back legs and run away as fast as you can.

When that occurs, where will you find the motivation and the strength to make your marriage a success? What will encourage and empower you to hang in there and do what you ought to do regardless of how you feel?

There's only one real answer to that question: A deep and vital relationship with Jesus Christ. This is the only thing that will give you strength and motivation to hang in there and solve your problems.

Jesus must be your support in times of trouble. He must be your trusted advisor and constant companion. He must be your ultimate reason for living. He must be your sufficiency, your all in all. He must be the One who enables you to keep your marriage comitment when the going gets tough.

What this means is that to have a marriage God's way, you must

Preparing
for Marriage
God's Way

make your relationship with Jesus Christ a priority matter. Never let anything or anyone come between you and your Lord! Never allow anything or anyone to pull you away from His arms of love.

Stay close to Him, come what may. Personally spend time each day in His Word and in prayer. Devote yourselves as a couple to regular practice of Bible study and worship. Dedicate yourselves to meeting faithfully with other believers to encourage and be encouraged, to minister and to receive ministry. Make involvement in a Biblical church a priority issue in your lives. "Draw near to God and he will draw near to you." (James 4:7)

Mark it down as a basic axiom for your marital success: **Your relationship with God is the most important relationship in your relationship with each other.** Make sure you don't neglect it.

This session has been planned to facilitate three primary goals. First, this session will aid you in personally evaluating and enlarging this most basic and important of all your relationships. Second, it will help you explore your similarities and differences in terms of your relationship with God and your spiritual convictions. Finally, it has been designed to assist you in developing a spiritual growth and development strategy for you as a married couple.

So roll up your sleeves, begin your effort with fervent prayer, put on your thinking cap, pick up your Bible and a pen, find a quiet place and go to work.

Begin by filling out the form entitled **Spiritual Convictions Questionnaire.** This will help you evaluate your own spiritual life. It will also help you see where the two of you are alike and different in your spiritual lives.

Next, work through the sheets entitled **Your Prayer Life** and **Your Bible Reading Or Bible Study Practice.**

Preparing for Marriage
God's Way

SPIRITUAL CONVICTIONS QUESTIONNAIRE

Finish the following sentences with two or three answers each.

1. God is _____
   _____
   _____

2. Jesus Christ is (describe who you think He is, what He has done, what He is doing now, what place He has in your life, what He means to you, etc.) _____
   _____
   _____

3. My relationship to God and his Son Jesus Christ is (describe the kind of relationship you have with God and how important that relationship is—be specific) _____
   _____
   _____

4. A Christian is _____
   _____
   _____

5. I know that I am (or am not) a Christian because _____
   _____
   _____

6. The Bible is (describe what you think it is, what it means to you, what place it has in your life, how you use it, etc.) _____
   _____
   _____

7. Sin is _____
   _____
   _____

8. My chief sins are _____
   _____
   _____

9. When I sin, I (describe how you handle sin, what you feel when you sin, what you do after you sin) _____
   _____
   _____

10. I feel guilty when _____
    _____
    _____

11. I pray (when, how, why, what for, etc.) _____

_____

_____

12. My chief goals in life are _____

_____

_____

13. I want (or do not want) to attend and be involved in church (answer the questions "how" and "why") _____

_____

_____

14. I believe fellowship with other Christians is (define what it is, what it involves, how important it is, and how it can be developed) _____

_____

_____

15. I am promoting my spiritual growth and the spiritual growth of my partner by _____

_____

_____

16. My partner and I differ in spiritual matters (when, how, over what, etc.) _____

_____

_____

17. The changes I would like to make in my own spiritual life are _____

_____

_____

18. The changes I would like my partner to make spiritually are _____

_____

_____

Review your answers. Are there any that you would like to change? Which ones? Why? Are there any to which you do not know the answer? Which ones? Compare and discuss your answers with your partner. Write down your impressions of this study. What have you learned about yourself and what have you learned about your partner? What changes do you need to make in light of this study?

YOUR PRAYER LIFE

A Self-Evaluation

1. How would you characterize your prayer life?

   a. Very satisfactory _____

   b. Satisfactory _____

   c. Satisfactory but needing improvement _____

   d. Unsatisfactory _____

   e. Very unsatisfactory _____

2. Briefly state your reasons for answering question 1 as you did.

   a. _____

   b. _____

   c. _____

   d. _____

   e. _____

3. On a scale from 0 to 10, with 10 being the highest rating, how important do you consider prayer in the Christian life _____?

4. On a scale from 0 to 10, how important is prayer in your actual practice _____?

5. If you think your prayer life should be improved, make a list of ways that you could improve your practice of prayer. Consider what hinders your prayer life and how those hindrances could be removed.

   a. _____

   b. _____

   c. _____

   d. _____

   e. _____

   f. _____

   g. _____

   h. _____

6. When and where do you pray? List the occasions (times) and locations (places).

   a. _____

   b. _____

   c. _____

d. _____

e. _____

f. _____

g. _____

7. Mark an X after each phrase describing an activity included in your prayers:

a. Adoration and worship of God _____

b. Praise to God _____

c. Petition (asking) for your own concerns _____

d. Petition (asking) for the concerns of your family _____

e. Petition (asking) for the concerns of your friends _____

f. Petition (asking) for missionaries _____

g. Petition (asking) for church leaders _____

h. Petition (asking) for church members _____

i. Petition (asking) for government officials (local and national) _____

j. Petition (asking) for the world scene _____

k. Confession of your sin _____

l. Petition (asking) for non-physical concerns (needs, desires) _____

m. Petition (asking) for physical concerns (needs, desires, wants) _____

n. Others _____

_____

8. Go back over the preceding list and identify the five activities that usually consume most of your prayer time. List these activities and assess whether you think you are emphasizing the things you should emphasize.

a. _____

b. _____

c. _____

d. _____

e. _____

9. Study Matthew 6:9-13 and write down everything you see in this passage about effective prayer.

a. _____

b. _____

c. _____

d. _____

e. _____

f. _____

g. _____

h. _____

10. Study Ephesians 1:15-19; 3:14-21; 6:18-20; Philippians 1:3-6; 1:9-11; Colossians 1:3-13 and list everything you see in these passages about effective prayer.

a. _____

b. _____

c. _____

d. _____

e. _____

f. _____

g. _____

h. _____

11. What personal challenges have you reached and what changes should you make in your practice of prayer as a result of the self-analysis of these passages and your own prayer life?

12. What can you and will you do to make sure these changes will actually become a reality in your prayer life?

a. _____

b. _____

c. _____

d. _____

YOUR BIBLE READING OR BIBLE STUDY PRACTICE

A Self-Evaluation

1. How would you characterize your Bible readings or Bible study practice?

    a. Very satisfactory _____

    b. Satisfactory _____

    c. Satisfactory, but needing improvement _____

    d. Unsatisfactory _____

    e. Very unsatisfactory _____

2. Briefly state your reasons for answering question 1 as you did.

    a. _____

    b. _____

    c. _____

    d. _____

    e. _____

3. On a scale from 0 to 10, with 10 being the highest rating, how important do you consider Bible reading or Bible study in the Christian life? _____

4. On a scale of 0 to 10, how important is Bible reading or Bible study in your actual practice? _____

5. If you think your Bible reading or Bible study practice should be improved, make a list of ways you could improve your Bible reading or Bible study. Consider what hinders your Bible reading or Bible study and how those hindrances could be removed.

    a. _____

    b. _____

    c. _____

    d. _____

    e. _____

    f. _____

    g. _____

    h. _____

6. When and where do you read or study your Bible? List the occasions (times) and locations (places).

    a. _____

b. _____

c. _____

d. _____

e. _____

f. _____

g. _____

7. Mark an X after each phrase describing a factor involved in your Bible reading or Bible study practice.

a. Regularity _____

b. Memorization _____

c. Meditation _____

d. Prayer before Bible study/Bible reading _____

e. Personal application of what you study _____

f. Looking up cross-references _____

g. Use of commentaries _____

h. Writing down your thoughts in a notebook for review and preservation _____

i. Finding a quiet place _____

j. Sharing what you learned with others _____

k. Use of different Bible translations _____

l. Personalization of what you learned _____

m. Prayer for help to live out what you learned _____

n. Asking others for help when you do not understand _____

o. Other _____

8. Study Joshua 1:8, 9; Ezra 7:10; Psalm 1:1-3; Psalm 19:7-11; Psalm 119:1-11, 72, 82, 92, 116, 127; Proverbs 6:20-23; Isaiah 8:19, 20; John 5:39, 40; John 17:17; Acts 17:11; Colossians 3:16; 2 Timothy 2:15; Hebrews 4:12; James 1:18-25.

Write down everything you see in these passages about Bible reading or Bible study.

a. _____

b. _____

c. _____

d. _____

e. _____

f. _____

g. _____

h. _____

i. _____

j. _____

k. _____

l. _____

m. _____

n. _____

o. _____

p. _____

9. What personal challenges have you received and what changes should you make in your Bible reading and Bible study practice as a result of a study of these passages and your self-evaluation?

a. _____

b. _____

c. _____

d. _____

e. _____

f. _____

g. _____

h. _____

i. _____

j. _____

k. _____

10. What can you and will you do to make sure these changes become a reality in your practice?

a. _____

b. _____

c. _____

d. _____

e. _____

f. _____

Session 6:
COMMUNICATING GOD'S WAY — Part 1

Preparing for marriage God's way will require you to devote your attention to the issue of your communication with each other. God is vitally concerned about this aspect of your relationship. Indeed, He says that He is grieved when there is a deficiency in this area of your life. (Ephesians 4:29,30).

But more than that, the depth and satisfaction of your relationship is dependent on how well you are doing in this area. You will never develop or maintain a marriage that approximates God's desires apart from an effective communication system.

In a sense, your communication may be seen as the life blood of the marriage relationship. In the human body, if something hinders the flow of the blood, the whole person suffers. So too, if something interferes with the flow of your communication, your whole relationship will reap the consequences.

Most marriage counselors will agree that a breakdown of communication is almost always involved in marital dysfunction. No one working in this realm disputes the fact that ineffective communication has disastrous results.

All sorts of unpleasant things may happen when people don't communicate effectively. Issues will remain unclarified. Wrong ideas will continue uncorrected. Conflicts and misunderstandings will be perpetuated. Confusion and disorder will occur. The development of deep unity, emotional closeness and intimacy will be hindered. Interpersonal problems pile up and barriers will become higher and wider. The temptation to look for someone else who will satisfy social desires may be encouraged. Wise decision making will be thwarted.

And these are just for starters. Without a doubt, proper communication is a key to establishing and maintaining a deep and satisfying marital relationship. Without it, you will be inhibited from developing a marriage that reflects God's beautiful plan for husbands and wives.

You may think that your communication system is working quite effectively. Perhaps you are convinced that this is one area in your relationship in which there is little room for improvement. Possibly, you're of the opinion that if it doesn't need fixing, don't fix it.

After all, you talk about everything. You share with one another freely. You are able to be lovingly honest about what you think and how you feel. You understand each other. You listen respectfully and respond appropriately. You are able to disagree and discuss your disagreements without becoming hurt or attacking one another. Your conversation is beneficial and uplifting.

Well, if these things are true of your relationship, **GREAT!** You're very fortunate. You're laying a good foundation for a successful relationship, because effective communication is a critical factor in developing a really good marriage.

Preparing for Marriage God's Way

Keep on doing whatever you are doing that is right. Don't become nonchalant. Never cease working on this facet of your relationship.

Our experience as marriage and family counselors has brought us into contact with many who say, "I don't know what has happened to us. We used to be able to communicate very well. We used to talk about everything. We enjoyed sharing. We kept no secrets. We could discuss disagreements. We listened to one another. We understood each other.

"But that's all different now. We don't seem to have anything to talk about. And when we do communicate, it often ends in disaster. We just don't seem to be on the same wavelength anymore."

This scenario may illustrate two things: First, it may indicate that these people were wrong about the way they assessed their previous communication system. It may not have been as effective as they thought it was. We sometimes tend to romanticize what takes place in courtship and the early stages of marriage.

Second, this scenario may demonstrate what happens when you neglect some activity in which you had developed some expertise. This may occur by default rather than design. Almost no one deliberately decides to neglect this area. It just happens.

But whether by design or default, the consequences are still the same. The couple drifts apart. The relationship deteriorates. Emotional closeness disappears. Basic communication skills and efforts degenerate.

So, even if communication is one of your strong points, take these studies on communication seriously. Using the words of the apostle Paul out of context, excel even more (1 Thessalonians 4:10). Remember, there's always room for improvement.

Effective communication is so important and complex that we are devoting two sessions to it in this book. In these two sessions, you will be challenged to evaluate your communication system, to explore certain aspects of what God has to say about communication in His Word and to practice the effective communication style prescribed therein.

Okay, it's time to roll up your sleeves, pray fervently, find a quiet place, pick up pen and Bible, put on your thinking cap and go to work on Session 6 exercises. First, do the **Communication Quality/Quantity Inventory** individually. Follow the instructions carefully. Be very honest about your perspective and desires. Then get together and discuss your answers. Write down the conclusions you reached. And, as always, record any questions for discussion that this exercise generates.

Having completed this assignment, move on to complete the **Practical Exercise For Nonverbal Communication.** Be aware that communication is more than words. It's done by the

Preparing for Marriage God's Way

expression on your face, the way you laugh, what you laugh at or don't laugh at, the way you use your hands or don't use your hands, the way you use your time or don't use your time, etc.

Whether you like it or not, you are communicating all the time by your nonverbal behavior. And you'd better believe that this nonverbal communication is powerful. In fact, if there's a contradiction between what people hear and what they see, they'll probably be inclined to believe what they see rather than what they hear.

So give your full attention to this assignment and learn what you can about the way you and your partner communicate. Get in touch with your own nonverbal language. Become sensitive to what signals and messages you're sending out. Recognize the power to build or destroy your nonverbal behavior has. Work on eliminating destructive signals and increasing positive, enriching messages.

Another important aspect of proper communication is knowing what to avoid in terms of what you actually say. The Scripture has a lot to say about the way you use your tongue. The Lord is quite clear about the wrong way to speak to and about one another. It is therefore important to understand what God has to say about the wrong way of using your tongue. Now, complete the worksheet to help you identify and eliminate any destructive speech patterns that you may be practicing.

Preparing for Marriage
God's Way

COMMUNICATION QUALITY/ QUANTITY INVENTORY

1. What does it mean to be able to communicate with another person? Define what you think constitutes effective communication.

_____

_____

_____

2. Consider the following items. Which ones do you communicate about? Rate the **quality** of your communication on each of these items as *Excellent; Good; Fair; Poor.* Rate the **quantity** of your communication on each of these items in terms of *Too Much; Just Right; Too Little; Nonexistent.*

	Quality Rating	/	Quantity Rating
1. Spiritual issues, church, Christian service, devotions		/	
2. Facts, information		/	
3. Ideas, opinions, judgments		/	
4. Desires, concerns, interests		/	
5. Feelings, emotions		/	
6. Plans, goals, purposes		/	
7. Expectations, aspirations		/	
8. Finances		/	
9. Work or school		/	
10. Family matters, parenting		/	
11. Dreams		/	
12. Sex		/	
13. Friends		/	
14. Recreation, sports		/	
15. Problems, failures, defeats		/	

16. Joys, victories, successes   _____ / _____

17. Current events   _____ _____ / _____

18. What you read, study   _____ / _____

19. TV or movies   _____ / _____

List the items in which you would like to improve your communication:

_____

_____

_____

List other items that could be included in your communication which are not listed previously:

_____

_____

_____

List items on which you find yourself in frequent disagreement with others. Why?

_____

_____

_____

Identify factors that have hindered effective communication for you and for others.

_____

_____

_____

PRACTICAL EXERCISE FOR NONVERBAL COMMUNICATION

1. Make a list of the following scripture references and then study (write down) what each one indicates about nonverbal communication.

Genesis 3:7-10 _____

Genesis 4:5-6 _____

Genesis 32:6, 7 _____

Genesis 37:3_____

Genesis 39:4 _____

Genesis 40:6-7 _____

Joshua 7:6 _____

1 Samuel 1:4-10 _____

1 Samuel 18:4 _____

1 Kings 19:3, 4a _____

1 Kings 21:4 _____

Proverbs 4:25, 26 _____

Proverbs 7:6-9 _____

Proverbs 7:10-13a _____

Proverbs 31:12-27 _____

Mark 2:3-5 _____

Luke 18:10-13 _____

Luke 10:30-35a _____

Luke 15:3-4, 8, 20 _____

1 John 3:17 _____

2. Practice communicating at least six of the following emotions, attitudes or issues in a nonverbal way. Do not say a word; just communicate by nonverbal means. Do not tell the other person what you are attempting to communicate. Let the other person guess. Alternate the exercise from one person to the next. Keep a record of how many times you accurately read what the other person was feeling or attempting to communicate.

Love	Anger
Happiness	Sexual Interest
Peace	Frustration
Uneasiness	Irritation
Fear	Discouragement
Sadness	Unbelief
Indifference	Doubt
Apathy	Humility
Anxiety	Guilt

Disinterest   Cautiousness
Hurt   Trust
Confidence   Pride

3. Discuss and write down what you learned from, or felt, while performing this exercise.

_____

_____

_____

4. Developing oneness in marriage requires communicating properly, both verbally and nonverbally.

   a. List at least 10 nonverbal ways of communicating with another person.

   1. _____

   2. _____

   3. _____

   4. _____

   5. _____

   6. _____

   7. _____

   8. _____

   9. _____

   10. _____

   b. List some nonverbal behaviors that may hinder the development of a deep and satisfying relationship in marriage.

   _____

   _____

   _____

   _____

   c. List some nonverbal behaviors that may enhance oneness and make marriage a satisfying experience.

   _____

   _____

   _____

d. Identify the nonverbal behaviors which you do that could hinder oneness.

_____

_____

_____

_____

_____

e. Identify the nonverbal behaviors which you do that encourage a good relationship.

_____

_____

_____

_____

_____

f. Discuss these items thoroughly with each other and write how you will improve your nonverbal communication.

_____

_____

_____

_____

_____

HOW TO BECOME AN EFFECTIVE COMMUNICATOR

A. Consider what happens when people don't communicate effectively. Try to think of illustrations from your own experience, from others or from the Bible.

1. Issues remain unclarified. (Proverbs 18:17)
2. Wrong ideas or assumptions are uncorrected.
3. Conflicts remain unresolved.
4. Confusion and disorder develop.
5. Wise decision making is thwarted.
6. The development of deep unity, intimacy and emotional closeness is hindered.
7. Interpersonal problems are intensified.
8. Boredom, discontentment and frustration with the relationship are fostered.
9. Spiritual growth, mutual sharpening and stimulation are impeded.
10. Shallow relationships, distancing, estrangement and drifting apart are promoted.
11. Bad attitudes toward, suspiciousness of the other person are nurtured.
12. Understanding each other deeply is prevented.

B. Reflect on the different means and facets of communication. Give illustrations of what and how you may communicate by these means.

1. Visually: with a wink, by staring, etc.
2. Verbally: what you say or don't say and how you say it.
3. By notes or letters.
4. By facial expressions: smiles or frowns, etc.
5. With your body: hand or feet motions, rigidity, etc.
6. By your presence or absence.
7. By a touch, a hug, a pat, a squeeze, a slap, a caress, etc.
8. By helping or not helping.
9. By giving or withholding a present.
10. By a willingness to share or an unwillingness to share.
11. By listening carefully and refusing to listen.
12. By seeking and accepting advice or by doing the opposite.
13. Other ways that you can think of:

_____

_____

_____

C. Think about the different levels or styles of communication. Give at least one example of ways you have or could communicate on each of these levels. Assess your own and your partner's communication on each of these levels in terms of: Very good (just right) — 2; Adequate but could stand some improvement — 1; Inadequate (too much + or too little –) – 0 + or 0 –. Identify ways in which you should improve.

	You	Partner
1. Cliche level: "Hello, how are you?", "Nice day, isn't it?"	_____	_____
2. Sharing facts or information about work, people, news events, your reading, etc.	_____	_____

3. Sharing ideas, opinions, thoughts, plans, and judgments: "I like. . .", "I don't like. . .", "I think. . .", "My view of this is. . .", "I want to. . ." _____ _____

4. Sharing feelings or emotions: "I am really sad about. . .", "Right now I am very discouraged or happy or whatever. . .", "I am really starting to get upset or angry or (?) about what has just happened or been said." _____ _____

5. Asking questions, exploring or interviewing: "What do you think about. . .", "Tell me about your day or (?)", "What do you really want to do?", "If you could do anything you wanted to do, what would it be?", "What has the Lord been teaching you recently?", "How can I improve. . ." _____ _____

6. Making suggestions: "Perhaps it would be a good idea to. . .", "In my opinion, you're trying to do too much." _____ _____

7. Giving support, appreciation, affirmation, comfort or encouragement: "I believe you can do it", "Thanks, I needed or wanted that", "You're doing a great job", "You have been such a blessing to me", "I was really helped by what you said about. . .", "I'm praying for you", "I see God at work in your life." _____ _____

8. Giving instruction or direction: "The Bible teaches. . .", "In Ephesians 4:25, God says. . .", "What that means is. . .", "You should. . ." _____ _____

9. Admonishing, correcting, confronting: "Here's an area of your thinking or life that you are neglecting", "At times you seem to be very irritated", "Sometimes when other people talk to you, you don't seem to be interested", "When you did or said such and such, I thought or felt that you were putting me down or rejecting me." _____ _____

10. Acknowledging sins and failures: "Please forgive me. What I did was wrong. I've asked God for forgiveness and now I'm asking you for the same. Will you forgive me?", "I really blew it that time. With God's help, I'll try to do better", "When I did thus and such, I was very inconsiderate and insensitive." _____ _____

11. Talking over plans and decisions. _____ _____

12. Making plans and decisions mutually. _____ _____

13. Discussing problems, disagreements, controversial issues. _____ _____

14. Praying together. _____ _____

15. Discussing Scripture, spiritual issues. _____ _____

16. Sharing the Gospel, the way God has and is blessing you. _____ _____

17. Giving praise to God. _____ _____

D. Make a list of the "circuit jammers" (hindrances to good communication) found in these verses.

1. Ephesians 4:25 _____

_____ ____

2. Ephesians 4:29 _____

_____ ____

3. Ephesians 4:31 _____

_____ ____

4. Colossians 3:8 _____

_____ ____

5. Colossians 3:9 _____

_____ ____

6. Proverbs 11:12 _____

_____ ____

7. Proverbs 11:13 _____

_____ ____

8. Proverbs 12:16 _____

_____ ____

9. Proverbs 12:18 _____

_____ ____

10. Proverbs 15:1 _____

_____ ____

11. Proverbs 15:5 _____

_____

_____

12. Proverbs 16:27 _____

_____

_____

13. Proverbs 17:9 _____

_____

_____

14. Proverbs 18:2 _____

_____

_____

15. Proverbs 18:6 _____

_____

_____

16. Proverbs 18:8 _____

_____

_____

17. Proverbs 18:13 _____

_____

_____

18. Proverbs 18:17 _____

_____

_____

19. Proverbs 18:23 _____

_____

_____

20. Proverbs 19:1 _____

_____

_____

21. Proverbs 19:5 _____

_____

_____

22. Proverbs 20:19 _____

_____

_____ _____

23. Proverbs 20:25 _____

_____

_____ _____

24. Proverbs 25:24 _____

_____

_____ _____

25. Proverbs 26:18, 19 _____

_____

_____ _____

26. Proverbs 26:20, 21 _____

_____

_____ _____

27. Proverbs 26:22 _____

_____

_____ _____

28. Proverbs 27:2 _____

_____

_____ _____

29. Proverbs 29:20 _____

_____

_____ _____

E. Review the list of hindrances to good communication you have noted in these passages. Evaluate yourself and your partner on each of the 29 items on this list to discern what you are doing well and how you need to improve. Use the rating scale: **Never do this — 4; Seldom do this—3; Sometimes do this—2; Frequently do this—1; Always do this—0.** Be honest about your ratings. Put your ratings on the lines provided on the right hand side of the page after each passage. Make this exercise a real learning experience. The higher your scores, the better will be your communication and your relationship.

F. Make a list of any of the hindrances on which you or your partner rated you 0, 1 or 2. Think about, pray about, discuss, plan what you can do to improve.

1. _____

2. _____

3. _____

4. _____

5. _____

6. _____

7. _____

8. _____

G. Read the following sentences and determine which of the principles listed under D they violate. Which circuit jammers do they illustrate?

1. You make me sick. _____

2. I hope you get what you deserve. _____

3. If you don't like it, you can lump it. _____

4. You never do a good job at anything you do. _____

5. I don't really care what you think. _____

6. You're going to be sorry. _____

7. I can't promise you what I'm going to do. _____

8. You are such a nit-wit, a real nincompoop. _____

9. Why don't you just shut up! _____

10. Whatever I set my mind to, I can do. _____

11. This time, I'm going to get even. _____

12. I'm going to teach you a real lesson. _____

13. Drop dead! _____

14. Let me tell you how it is. _____

15. Just be quiet and let me tell you what you should do. I don't need to hear anymore. _____

16. Why in the world would you ever do something like that! _____

17. If you were a real woman or man, you. . . _____

18. I know I promised to do it, but. . . _____

19. You're making a big deal out of nothing. _____

20. Anybody knows it's not the way you say it is. _____

21. After what you've done, you expect me to love you? _____

22. Let me tell you about what so and so did. _____

23. I've talked to you about this a million times. _____

24. Here we go again! _____

25. I don't want to hear about your problems. I've got enough of my own. _____

26. You don't care at all about what I think. _____

27. I know you said. . ., but this is what's really happening. _____

28. No one else understands it or can do it as well as I. _____

29. You're never satisfied. You're the one who is causing problems. _____

30. It's all your fault. _____

31. Why don't you get off your high horse! _____

32. So I lied. Don't make such a big deal out of it. _____

33. You should have known I didn't really mean it. Anybody knows I was only kidding. You just take things too seriously. _____

H. Go back over this list and put a circle around the number of any of the statements that are similar to ones that you have made. Put a check mark in front of the statements that are similar to ones that you have heard your partner make. Discuss the impact of such statements on you, your relationship and others. Pray and work on eliminating such statements from your conversation.

Session 7:
COMMUNICATING GOD'S WAY — Part 2

In session 6, you explored the key issues of nonverbal communication and communication hindrances. In this session, you will be discussing two more important aspects.

Now that you have seen what to avoid (the circuit jammers), it will be meaningful to explore what the Scripture has to say about what helps or promotes good communication. The worksheet entitled **How To Become An Effective Communicator** and **Twelve Practical Suggestions For Developing And Maintaining Good Marital Communications** will facilitate such a study. So put on your learning cap and let God teach you.

Good listening is an important part of effective communication. Talking is not necessarily the same as communicating. Talking involves sending a message. Communicating includes accurately *receiving* the message as well. It involves people coming to a common meaning so that both sender and receiver are drawn together and mutually enriched and encouraged (Ephesians 4:25, 29).

For this to occur, there must be good listening and good speaking. Scripture has much to say about the foolishness of answering a matter before we have listened. Yet, often we are so busy talking or planning how to respond that we don't really listen to the other person. As a result, we don't communicate effectively and we don't relate deeply. The **Listening Quotient Inventory** will help you explore this vital area of your relationship.

To conclude and draw all of your studies on communication together, fill out the checklist entitled, **Communication Checklist.**

When you come to the class/counseling session, be prepared to share your honest feedback or questions about what has transpired in your study time or the class sessions. Be ready to share how the principles you are learning apply to your lives and relationship, how you have implemented the principles or failed to do so.

Preparing for Marriage God's Way

HOW TO BECOME AN
EFFECTIVE COMMUNICATOR

A. Make a list of things that you can share with your partner.

1. _____
2. _____
3. _____
4. _____
5. _____
6. _____
7. _____
8. _____
9. _____
10. _____

B. Make a list of helps to good communication found in the following verses.

1. Ephesians 4:15, 25 _____
2. Ephesians 4:29 _____
3. Ephesians 4:26, 27 _____
4. Ephesians 4:32 _____
5. Ephesians 5:33 _____
6. Psalm 141:3 _____
7. Isaiah 8:10, 20 _____
8. Matthew 19:3 ,4 _____
9. Isaiah 50:4 _____
10. Ecclesiastes 12:10 _____
11. Proverbs 12:25 _____
12. Proverbs 15:1 _____
13. Proverbs 15:2 _____
14. Proverbs 15:28 _____
15. Proverbs 16:23, 24 _____
16. Proverbs 17:14 _____
17. Proverbs 18:23 _____
18. Proverbs 20:5 _____
19. Proverbs 20:15 _____

20. Proverbs 25:9 _____

21. Proverbs 25:11, 12 _____

22. Proverbs 25:15 _____

23. Proverbs 29:11 _____

24. Proverbs 31:26 _____

25. Galatians 5:13 _____

26. Romans 13:7, 8 _____

27. Proverbs 5:18, 19 _____

28. 1 Peter 3:1-7 _____

C. List at least 10 important communication enhancers, promoters or facilitators that you found in these verses.

1. _____
2. _____
3. _____
4. _____
5. _____
6. _____
7. _____
8. _____
9. _____
10. _____

D. List three times or situations when you have not communicated well. Using the guidelines from the previous verses analyze these incidents to discern what you could have done that would have been more effective.

1. _____
2. _____
3. _____

E. Using the following list as headings, list three items under each in order of priority as you believe your partner would respond: His/her joys; disappointments; goals; dislikes; interests; concerns. Ask your partner to check your knowledge of him/her.

Joys

1. _____
2. _____
3. _____

Disappointments

    1. _____

    2. _____

    3. _____

Goals

    1. _____

    2. _____

    3. _____

Dislikes

    1. _____

    2. _____

    3. _____

Interests

    1. _____

    2. _____

    3. _____

Concerns

    1. _____

    2. _____

    3. _____

F. Make a list of at least ten fun things your partner enjoys which you can enjoy together. Plan to do at least one each week.

    1. _____

    2. _____

    3. _____

    4. _____

    5. _____

    6. _____

    7. _____

    8. _____

    9. _____

   10. _____

G. List the personal insights and challenges you have received from this study. Be personal and specific.

1. _____
2. _____
3. _____
4. _____
5. _____
6. _____
7. _____
8. _____
9. _____
10. _____

TWELVE PRACTICAL SUGGESTIONS FOR DEVELOPING AND MAINTAINING GOOD MARITAL COMMUNICATIONS

Rating Scale: Always — 4; Often — 3; Sometimes — 2; Seldom — 1; Never — 0.

	You	Mate

1. When there are problems, each must be willing to admit that he/she is part of the problem. (Genesis 3:8-19; Proverbs 20:6) _____ _____

2 Each person must be willing to change. (John 5:6; Matthew 5:23-26) _____ _____

3. Avoid the use of emotionally charged words. "You don't really love me." "You always do . . ." "You never do anything right." "I don't care." _____ _____

4. Be responsible for your own emotions, words, actions, and reactions. Don't blame them on the other person. You got angry, lashed out, became depressed, etc. (Galatians 6:5; James I:13-15) _____ _____

5. Refrain from having reruns on old arguments. (Ephesians 4:26) _____ _____

6. Deal with one problem at a time. Solve one problem and then move on to the next. (Matthew 6:34 principle) _____ _____

7. Deal in the present and not in the past. Hang a "no fishing" sign over the past unless it will help you to solve your present problems. (Philippians 3:12-14; Jeremiah 31:34; Isaiah 43:25) _____ _____

8. Major on the positive instead of majoring on the negative. (Philippians 4:8) _____ _____

9. Learn to communicate in nonverbal ways. (Matthew 8:1, 2, 14, 15; Psalm 32:8) _____ _____

10. Express your thoughts and concerns to each other. Relate your activities. Listen, understand, and respond to the meaning behind what a person is saying. When he flies off the handle at you, he may be saying, "I've had a terrible day at the job. Nobody respects me." When he says, "You don't love me," he may be really saying, "I desperately need some affection. I'm starved for love." (Example of Jesus in John 1:45-47; Mark 5:1-15; John 11:20-35) _____ _____

11. Practice the golden rule—Matthew 7:12. What would you like your mate to do to you? Would you like your mate to: Tell you the truth? Ask your opinion? Help in time of need? Be natural around you? Thank you for your help or services? Well, then do the same for him. _____ _____

12. Practice the principle laid down in Luke 6:35. "Do good—do that which will help others; and lend expecting and hoping for nothing in return." _____ _____

LISTENING QUOTIENT INVENTORY

Listening well is a very important part of effective communication and an essential element in developing deep, Godly relationships. To discover your "listening quotient" (i.e., how well you are doing as a listener), complete the following inventory and then ask a close friend who will give you honest feedback to do the same. Circle the appropriate number representing your listening behavior for each statement.

Rating scale: Usually = 3; Sometimes = 2; Seldom = 1; Never = 0.

1. I realize that listening is an important aspect of ministering to another person: 3   2   1   0.

2. When someone else is speaking to me, I pay close attention to that person and don't allow my mind to wander: 3   2   1   0.

3. I don't close my mind to what the other person is saying even if it differs with my own ideas; I am willing to learn and evaluate what I hear; and I speak Biblically: 3   2   1   0.

4. I don't stop listening to the other person even if he/she is saying something I don't want to hear: 3   2   1   0.

5. People who know me would say I am a good listener: 3   2   1   0.

6. I refrain from judging what the other person has said until I'm sure I have understood what he/she means. I do not jump to conclusions: 3   2   1   0.

7. I realize the other person knows what he/she meant better than I do: 3   2   1   0.

8. I refrain from predicting what the other person is going to say: 3   2   1   0.

9. I refuse to use the time when the other person is speaking to prepare my rebuttal. I concentrate on trying to understand what the other person is saying, feeling and thinking rather than on my response to what is being said: 3   2   1   0.

10. I'm willing to be rebuked, criticized, or challenged without defending myself or immediately and excessively explaining myself: 3   2   1   0.

11. I withhold glib and hasty advice: 3   2   1   0.

12. I refrain from apologizing too quickly to get the other person to stop talking, resulting in his thinking I am not sincere and I really do not understand his feelings: 3   2   1   0.

13. I'm slow to correct the other person's evaluation of an issue: 3   2   1   0.

14. I hesitate to tell the other person how he should or should not feel about a matter: 3   2   1   0.

15. When someone else has spoken, I can accurately summarize and reflect what has been said: 3   2   1   0.

16. When another person is speaking, I refuse to interrupt; I am a patient listener: 3   2   1   0.

17. When someone else is speaking, I listen with my whole being (eyes, mind, ears, hands, feet, body posture, thoughts, inner man and outer man): 3   2   1   0.

Study the following verses and write down what each of them has to say about listening, hearing, paying attention, being quiet:

Genesis 21:17, 18 _____

Exodus 2:23, 24 _____

Exodus 22:25-27 _____

Psalm 6:3-9 _____

Job 21:1, 2 _____

Job 31:35 _____

Proverbs 1:5, 8, 33 _____

Proverbs 2:1, 2 _____

Proverbs 4:1, 10, 20 _____

Proverbs 5:1, 2 _____

Proverbs 8:6, 7, 32, 33 _____

Proverbs 10:8, 14 _____

Proverbs 12:15 _____

Proberbs 13:1 _____

Proverbs 15:31 _____

Proverbs 17:1, 4 _____

Proverbs 18:2, 13, 15 _____

Proverbs 19:20, 27 _____

Proverbs 25:12 _____

Proverbs 29:20 _____

Isaiah 30:15; 32:17 _____

Amos 5:13 _____

John 11:41, 42 _____

1 Thessalonians 4:11, 12 _____

1 Timothy 2:2 _____

James 1:19 _____

1 Peter 3:4 _____

Apply what you have learned this inventory and Bible study by completing the following statements:

By God's grace I am a good listener in these ways:

_____

_____

_____

With God's help I need to work on improving my listening skills in these ways and areas:

_____

_____

_____

_____

To improve my listening skills, I will:

_____

_____

_____

_____

COMMUNICATION CHECKLIST
(Used by permission of Rev. James Petty)

Rate both yourself and your partner on a scale of 1 to 5 on each of the following qualities of Biblical communication.

1 = very weak; 2 = weak; 3 = fair; 4 = good; 5 = excellent

	You	Partner
1. Does not lie. (Ephesians 4:25, Proverbs 12:19)	_____	_____
2. Is not evasive, but willing to share everything. (Ephesians 4:25)	_____	_____
3. Never flatters.	_____	_____
4. Speaks and does not clam up when under pressure or attack. (Ephesians 4:25)	_____	_____
5. Lets someone know in a controlled way why he/she is angry with that person. (Ephesians 4:26)	_____	_____
6. If bothered by someone, immediately finds time to discuss it with the offending party.	_____	_____
7. Is able to constructively discuss a problem one is angry about.	_____	_____
8. Does not say anything in an unloving way to someone who may be wrong.	_____	_____
9. Does not say anything in a disrespectful way to someone who may be wrong.	_____	_____
10. Does not use God's name in frustration, bitterness, rage or irritation. (Ephesians 4:29)	_____	_____
11. Does not say things to hurt others or make another feel bad. (Ephesians 4:29)	_____	_____
12. Says things in a way calculated to help the other person understand that he/she did wrong and gives the person hope for improvement.	_____	_____
13. Only says things that help in a conflict situation, not things that make it worse.	_____	_____
14. Always conditions criticism with some note of appreciation for legitimate strengths.	_____	_____
15. Does not react emotionally when verbally ignored, attacked, frustrated, etc. (Proverbs 15:1, Ephesians 4:31, 32)	_____	_____

16. Acts to diffuse conflict situations by a kind word or inquiry, in a spirit of reconciliation. (Proverbs 15:1) _____ _____

17. Communicates with God in prayer every day. _____ _____

18. Communicates honestly with God. _____ _____

19. Shares significant events, concerns, each day with partner to the extent he/she desires to hear those things. _____ _____

20. Desires to pray each day with partner about common concerns, praises. _____ _____

21. Spends time with God, focusing on listening to God's Word in Scriptures. _____ _____

22. Able to speak God's Word in a situation in such a way that it produces encouragement, hope, and greater strength. (Isaiah 50:4; Proverbs 12:18, 25) _____ _____

23. Thinks carefully before speaking in tense situations. (Proverbs 15:28; 16:23; 29:20) _____ _____

24. Is able to diffuse an argument by graciously dropping a matter when it is producing a quarrel. (Proverbs 17:4) _____ _____

25. Does not answer harshly to those over whom he/she has power. (Proverbs 18:23) _____ _____

26. Able and willing to draw out the feelings and thoughts of others close to him/her. (Proverbs 20:5; 1 Peter 3:7) _____ _____

27. Only speaks when well informed or knowledgeable about what should be said. (Proverbs 20:15; 18:2) _____ _____

28. Does not speak about people in a way that betrays confidence or belittles them before others. (Proverbs 25:9; 11:13; 17:9; 18:8; 26:22) _____ _____

29. Able to rebuke others when needed. (Proverbs 25:12; Romans 15:14) _____ _____

30. Able and willing to communicate the gospel or other Scripture as needed. (Proverbs 31:26) _____ _____

31. Speaks respectfully about and to those in authority. (Romans 13:7) _____ _____

32. Conversations often include words of delight and appreciation concerning one's partner.   _____ _____

33. Listens carefully and attentively when rebuked or criticized. (Proverbs 15:5; 18:13)   _____ _____

34. Keeps verbal promises. (Proverb 20:25; 26:18, 19)   _____ _____

35. Knows when and how to bring up a disagreement so that a contentious spirit is not projected. (Proverbs 25:24; 26:21)   _____ _____

36. Does not hurt people in jest.   _____ _____

37. Usually speaks in a way that others respect. (Proverbs 28:2)   _____ _____

38. Is never afraid to speak up to those who disagree and to take a stand when important issues are at stake.   _____ _____

RESOLVING CONFLICTS GOD'S WAY

One thing is for sure—a Christian home is not a home without problems and conflicts. In his commentary on Matthew 18:7, John Trapp says it is as unlikely that you could strike two pieces of flint together and not have sparks as it is that you could put two sinners together and not have conflicts.

The truth is that whenever two people enter into a really close relationship, some disagreements are inevitable. They are bound to occur.

Probably, the two of you already know that from personal experience in your relationship. If you don't, you will. You will have differences of opinion on certain issues, or else one of you doesn't do any thinking.

Disagreements are not necessarily bad. If there are not too many of them, they can be very helpful. If they are faced and handled God's way, they can have a positive impact rather than a negative one.

In fact, many couples who respond to their differences in a Biblical way often find that these disagreements stimulate growth and development in their lives and relationship. Contrasting or diverse viewpoints at first may appear to be monsters to be greatly feared. Later, when confronted and handled God's way, they turn out to be friends in disguise.

In this session, you'll see that God says conflicts may be resolved when people are willing to deal with them His way. You'll also note that God is very realistic in terms of what He *doesn't say* about conflict resolution.

Nowhere does the Bible indicate that conflict resolution comes naturally. For some reason, it's often easier to fight and argue than to want to be a peacemaker. It's often more natural to provoke and prolong than to pacify contention. When disagreements arise, how inclined we are to bite and devour rather than love (Galatians 5:13-16).

God doesn't suggest that resolving conflicts is "a piece of cake." Rather, He acknowledges that it's sometimes very difficult to come to agreement (Proverbs 18:19). It often requires a lot of work and effort. Though conflict resolution may be difficult, God makes it clear that with His help it isn't impossible. It doesn't come easily, but it can come if you will carefully follow His directives.

Fortunately, God's directives for resolving conflicts are given in abundant fashion in His Word. In this area, you don't need to thrash around on your own trying to find the best way to deal with the situation. It's not necessary for you to depend upon the fallible and often conflicting views of men. You can turn to God's infallible Word and discover His practical conflict resolution guidelines. And you can be assured that if anything will work, they will.

Preparing for Marriage God's Way

In this session, you will be exposed to some of these directives. Take them seriously. Do the assignments carefully. One day, perhaps today, you'll be glad you did.

Now seek God's help in prayer, find a quiet place, pick up Bible and pen, put on your thinking cap and go to work on the following assignments.

(1) Do the worksheet entitled **Biblical Help For Preventing, Avoiding, Restraining And Overcoming Strife And Contention** (Select at least 15 verses to study at this time; if you choose, you may look up the other verses at another time);

(2) Work through the **Guidelines For Good Conflict Resolution** worksheet;

(3) Fill out the form, **Conflict Analysis;**

(4) Complete the **Worksheet On Problem Solving;**

(5) Read and follow the instructions on the **Sorting Out Responsibilities** worksheet;

(6) Write a one or two page summary of your responses to these assignments; what you have learned about yourself, your partner; your relationship; how you were challenged; areas in which you need to improve and areas in which you are doing well; questions you would like to ask; issues about conflict resolution or other matters you would like to discuss.

Preparing for Marriage
God's Way

BIBLICAL HELP FOR PREVENTING, AVOIDING, RESTRAINING AND OVERCOMING STRIFE AND CONTENTION

1. Ask God for help (Matthew 7:7-9; James 4:2-3)

2. Carefully study the following passages and write down everything you see in them about strife, fighting, quarreling and contention. Look at each passage and identify if you can:

   a. Why people fight and/or quarrel.

   _____

   _____

   b. What it says about why you get into quarrels.

   _____

   _____

   c. What it says about a person who quarrels and/or fights and what it calls that person.

   _____

   _____

   d. The consequences of quarreling and/or fighting.

   _____

   _____

   e. What must be done to restrain and overcome strife and contention (be specific).

   _____

   _____

3. Choose several verses to memorize. Write them on 3 X 5 cards and work on memorizing them.

4. Select three times when you have been involved in a strife situation and, using the information from your Bible study on strife, analyze and:

   a. Write what you did that was Biblical;

   _____

   _____

   b. The ways in which you erred;

   _____

   _____

   c. Write what you could have done differently;

   _____

   _____

d. Imagine (picture) yourself actually following Biblical directions in the situation;

_____

_____

e. Pray about the situation (confess sin, ask for specific help, thank God that He will give it).

_____

_____

5. Keep a daily conflict or strife journal:

a. Record the facts — what happened, what was said and done, how you felt, what was the outcome.
b. Analyze what you did or said that was Biblical and/or un-Biblical.
c. Write out other things you could have done that would have been in harmony with Scripture.

PASSAGES:

Proverbs 10:12
Proverbs 13:10
Proverbs 15:1, 4, 18
Proverbs 16:32
Proverbs 17:14, 27
Proverbs 18:6, 19
Proverbs 19:11, 13
Proverbs 20:3
Proverbs 21:9, 19

Proverbs 25:8
Proverbs 26:17, 21
Proverbs 29:20, 22
Genesis 13:8, 9
Genesis 26:17-31
Judges 8:1-3
Judges 12:1-3
Ecclesiastes 10:4
II Samuel 19:41-43

II Samuel 10:1-14
II Kings 14:1-8
Jeremiah 28:1-11
Daniel 1:8-16
Romans 12:14-21
Romans 13:12-14
Colossians 3:12-15
I Timothy 6:1-4
James 3:14-4:2
James 4:2

GUIDELINES FOR GOOD CONFLICT RESOLUTION

This exercise will help you discern the kind of marriage partners the two of you may be. It is a list of what you and your partner should be doing when you have disagreements.

Read each statement. Then on the blank lines, record the number that corresponds to how often you and your partner practice this rule for effective conflict resolution. Use this scale:

"I never do this"	= 4	"I seldom do this"	= 3
"I sometimes do this"	= 2	"I frequently do this"	= 1
"I always do this"	= 0		

	YOU	PARTNER
1. When a disagreement or problem arises, I focus on what is happening and what I should do to correct it instead of trying to understand what my partner does.	____	____
2. When a problem arises, I am ready to admit that I may be part of the problem. I focus on what I am doing wrong, rather than on what my partner is doing wrong.	____	____
3. I realize I cannot change my partner; that he/she must want to change or all my efforts will compound the problem rather than solve the problem.	____	____
4. I realize that love is not primarily a feeling, but actions calculated to serve, please and help my partner in a God-honoring way.	____	____
5. I focus my attention on changing my own behavior, attitudes, reactions and responses toward my partner. I plan specific, attainable, repeatable, positive changes I can make.	____	____
6. I am constantly working to develop and maintain a good communication system. I know that relationships are hindered when there is no communication or the wrong kind of communication.	____	____
7. I am working to develop and maintain many commonalities with my partner, including common projects, common interests and common recreational activities. I do a variety of activities with him/her. I am creative in the expression of my love and appreciation of him/her.	____	____
8. I recognize and allow for differences between my partner and me. I know men and women tend to view things differently.	____	____
9. I regularly practice the Golden Rule as stated in Matthew 7:12. I treat my partner as I want to be treated.	____	____
10. I major on the positive qualities of my partner and our relationship rather than focus on the negative. I emphasize our commonalities rather than our differences. (Philippians 4:8)	____	____

11. I practice the principle laid down in Luke 6:34-35. I give and serve, expecting nothing in return.   _____   _____

12. I keep current. I deal with one problem at a time. I don't continue to have reruns on arguments from the past. I forgive and forget. (Matthew 6:34; Ephesians 4:26)   _____   _____

13. I try to maintain a close relationship with God through Jesus Christ. (John 14:6; I John 4:21; Matthew 22:37-39; Ephesians 5:21-33)   _____   _____

After you finish this exercise, count the number of 0 and 1 answers you gave and mark the number on the appropriate line below. Next, count the number of answers you gave with the numbers 2, 3 or 4. Record that number on the appropriate line below.

	YOU	PARTNER
Number of 0 and 1 answers	_____	_____
Number of 2, 3 and 4 answers	_____	_____

This exercise describes thirteen principles for good conflict resolution in your relationship with your partner and in your dealings with other people. It describes how you can be the kind of marriage partner God wants you to be. If you honestly answered several of the statements with a 2, 3 or 4, plan how you can change in order to answer those statements with a 0 or a 1. The more 0's and 1's you have, the better will be your relationship with your partner and with others. If you are behaving one way toward your partner and another way with others, chances are that after you are married, you will begin to treat your spouse the way you treat others.

CONFLICT ANALYSIS

Most couples have disagreements and conflicts in their relationships. Indicate below the approximate extent of agreement or disagreement there is between you and your partner for each item in the list. Use this scale:

1 — Always agree.   4 — Frequently disagree.
2 — Frequently agree.   5 — Almost always disagree.
3 — Occasionally disagree.   6 — Always disagree.

Circle the numbers of the items that are sources of great trouble or serious concern for you.

1. Use of money. _____

2. Recreational matters. _____

3. Spiritual matters. _____

4. Friends (social life). _____

5. Demonstrations of affection. _____

6. Correct or proper behavior. _____

7. Philosophy of life. Goals in life. _____

8. Time spent together. _____

9. Making major decisions. _____

10. Leisure time, interests and activities. _____

11. Career decisions. _____

12. Praying and Bible study together. _____

13. Where we will live after we are married. _____

14. What type of housing we will live in and our ideas of what type of housing we will _____ want in the future.

15. Ways of dealing with parents and future in-laws. _____

16. Use of alcohol or drugs. _____

17. How to resolve disagreements. _____

On a scale from 0 to 10, (0 = lowest; 10 = highest), indicate your overall satisfaction _____ level with your present relationship.

WORKSHEET ON PROBLEM SOLVING

List below the solutions to at least five problems that you have solved together God's way. These should be problems where you have had differences of opinion, difficult decisions to make, arguments, or personal antagonisms to overcome.

Problem Number One:

a. Define clearly.

_____

_____

_____

b. What does the Bible say about the problem?

_____

_____

_____

c. Determine practical ways for implementing Biblical principles in solving this problem.

_____

_____

_____

Problem Number Two:

a. Define clearly.

_____

_____

_____

b. What does the Bible say about the problem?

_____

_____

_____

c. Determine practical ways for implementing Biblical principles in solving this problem.

_____

_____

Problem Number Three:

a. Define clearly.

_____

_____

_____

b. What does the Bible say about the problem?

_____

_____

_____

c. Determine practical ways for implementing Biblical principles in solving this problem.

_____

_____

_____

Problem Number Four:

a. Define clearly.

_____

_____

_____

b. What does the Bible say about the problem?

_____

_____

_____

c. Determine practical ways for implementing Biblical principles in solving this problem.

_____

_____

_____

Problem Number Five:

a. Define clearly.

_____

_____

_____

b. What does the Bible say about the problem?

_____

_____

_____

c. Determine practical ways for implementing Biblical principles in solving this problem.

_____

_____

_____

SORTING OUT RESPONSIBILITIES

A Plan For Promoting Unity In Marriage
and Overcoming Marital Conflicts

Many times conflicts arise in marriage because there has been no clear delineation of responsibilities. Sometimes when everything is everybody's responsibility, everything becomes nobody's responsibility. Or everybody is trying to do the same thing and confusion, frustration, bitterness, and competitiveness are the result. One person has one view about how or when something should be done; and the other person has another; and neither is willing to yield. Or, one person always seems to do the yielding. This provides the soil in which sinful and unnecessary resentment and bitterness may develop.

Much of this conflict can be eliminated if clear lines of responsibility are delineated. The husband under God is the head or manager of the home (Ephesians 5:22-27; I Timothy 3:4, 5). He is the one who is finally responsible to lovingly and Biblically guide the home. The buck stops with him. But he may decide to let his wife (his chief helper — Genesis 2:18; Proverbs 31:10-31) take the leadership responsibility in certain areas. Indeed, he will be wise to do this because she most certainly has more gifts, abilities and insight and experience in some areas than he does. In other areas, he will be more gifted and capable than she, and there he should take the lead in making decisions.

The husband and wife should share insights and advice in every area, but someone ought to be given the responsibility of seeing that things get done. Look over the following list and decide who will have the responsibility to plan and implement the different areas. Remember, some things are not right or wrong—just different ways of doing things or different ways of looking at something. In areas which are not vitally important or clearly spelled out in Scripture, be willing to defer to the other person. Don't make mountains out of molehills! Don't make everything a major issue! Talk matters over, assign responsibilities, make decisions, support each other, help carry out decisions.

This sorting out responsibilities does not mean that a given area is one person's exclusive responsibility. It means that when a difference of opinion arises, one person has authority to make the choice. Certainly, in most areas a full and frank discussion will be conducted, all options and alternatives, pros and cons considered. However, when a conflict of opinion arises, someone must be allowed to make the decision, even if that decision is to wait until God brings the two of you into agreement. "If a house is divided against itself, that house will not be able to stand" (Mark 3:25, NASB).

In making a decision, make sure that you do not violate a Biblical principle. Seek the opinion and insight of your mate, ask God in prayer to guide you, believe that He will, consider and evaluate all options, and then, if you are the person who is responsible, make the decision. The other person should support the decision wholeheartedly and seek to make the decision a success unless it clearly violates Biblical principle. Unity in marriage (Genesis 2:24) is tremendously important and should be maintained carefully. Following this plan is one way of promoting this unity. However, it will work only if both people agree to abide by it.

This "sorting out responsibilities" does not mean the husband relinquishes his Biblical responsibility to be the loving leader of the family. What it does mean is that he recognizes that God has given his wife certain abilities and capacities which may make her more competent in some areas than he is. Thus he delegates to her responsibilities which are in keeping with her resources. All the while, he maintains veto power, but he will not use it unless his wife's decisions clearly violate Biblical principle.

Scripture declares: "[Love] is not rude; it is not self seeking" (1 Corinthians 13:5, NIV). "Make my joy complete by being like minded, having the same love, being one in spirit and purpose. Do nothing out of selfish ambition or vain conceit, but in humility consider others better than yourselves. Each of you should look not only to your own interests, but also to the interests of others" (Philippians 2:2-4, NIV). "Live in harmony with one another. Don't be proud, but be willing to associate with people of low position. Do not be conceited." "Be devoted to one another in brotherly love. Honor one another above yourselves" (Romans 12:16, 10, NIV). "If you keep on biting and devouring each other,. . . you will be destroyed by each other." "You, my brothers, were called to be free. But do not use your freedom to indulge your sinful nature; rather serve one another in love" (Galatians 5:15, 12, NIV).

This "Sorting Out Responsibilities" plan is offered as a means of actualizing these Bible admonitions.

SORTING OUT RESPONSIBILITIES CHECKLIST

On the blank space following the descriptive phrase, indicate who will be mainly responsible for the area described:

1. Children:

Neatness _____	Rules and Regulations _____
Bedtimes _____	Activities _____
Discipline _____	Social life (friends, dating) _____
Clothing _____	Allowances (money management) _____
Chores _____	Manners _____
School work _____	TV watching _____
Hygiene _____	Spiritual Life _____
Other ( ) _____	Other ( ) _____

2. Money Management (establishing budget) _____

3. Financing and bookkeeping (paying bills, keeping records) _____

4. Money raising _____

5. Purchasing food and household _____

6. Menu planning and cooking (dietician and chef) _____

7. Housecleaning _____

8. Spiritual oversight (church selection, attendance, family goals, family devotions, etc.) _____

9. Family activities (fun times, recreation, family projects, supervision of family nights) _____

10. Vacation plans _____

11. Clothing purchasing _____

12. Clothing maintenance _____

13. Automobile (selection, maintenance, etc.) _____

14. Savings account _____

15. Hospitality (friends in for dinner, etc.) _____

16. Investment planning _____

17. Real estate purchases (home selection, etc.) _____

18. Gift planning and purchasing _____

19. Memorabilia keeping (family records, pictures, newspaper clippings, letters, etc.) _____

20. Family photography _____

21. Special events (birthdays, anniversaries, etc.) _____

22. Furniture (selection, purchases, and maintaining) _____

23. Time and schedule organizing _____

24. Travel (motel, maps, directions, etc.) _____

25. Retirement (plans and provisions) _____

26. Yard work _____

27. Gardening _____

28. Family health services _____

29. Occupation, career _____

Add any other responsibilities you can think of, under 30-32.

30. _____

31. _____

32. _____

Session 9:
HUSBANDING GOD'S WAY

Everyone marries with certain ideas or expectations about many different issues in marriage. If the husband and wife have the same perspectives, harmony and bliss may occur. On the other hand, if their concepts are different and strongly held, division and misery may result.

People make at least three mistakes in their marital concepts and expectations: (1) Before marriage, a couple often *assumes* that they agree on various issues and thus never discuss them in detail. (2) They know that they have some disagreements, but think they aren't important. (Actually, they don't even know how much they disagree; nor can they resolve their differences because they have never talked about them.) And (3) They pretend they are in agreement with the other person when in reality they are not.

Thus they deceive themselves and others by refusing to admit what they really think. They are so intent on preventing any disturbances in their relationship that they portray a pseudo-mutuality.

On the surface, they give the impression that they agree completely; but in fact, mutuality does not exist. Sooner or later, in one way or another, under the real life situation in marriage, they are forced to be honest. At some time after the wedding day, reality forces itself upon them.

When their hopes are not fulfilled, each of them experiences disappointment because the other person has let them down. Or, they are saddened and frustrated because demands are being made of them that they perceive as unreasonable and excessive.

As has already been suggested in previous sessions, it is crucial that you and your partner explore the issue of husband/wife expectations thoroughly and come to some agreement on these matters. Sessions 8 and 9 will bring about discussion and agreement about crucial issues in your relationship.

In fulfilling the assignments in these chapters, you will be given a chance to:

(1) search out your own ideas concerning the roles and responsibilities of husbands and wives in marriage;

(2) come to a fuller understanding of what your partner thinks about this subject;

(3) search the Scriptures to get a fuller knowledge of what God says about these issues;

(4) compare and adjust your own expectations to God's good, perfect and well-pleasing directives;

(5) discuss all of these important concepts thoroughly.

So roll up your sleeves, pray fervently for God's help, find a quiet place, pick up Bible and pen, put on your thinking cap and go to work on the following assignments.

(If there is anything that you do not understand or with which

Preparing for Marriage
God's Way

you are not in agreement, write it down and bring it with you to counseling or the class session. Talk it over in the session with your counselor/teacher.)

1. You and your partner each write a **brief article** built on the phrases: "An Ideal Husband is. . ." and "In Marriage, I think the husband should. . ." In the article, be specific, practical, clear, concrete and as thorough as possible. Study Ephesians 5:25-33; I Peter 3:7, 8; I Timothy 3:4, 5; I Timothy 5:8; Colossians 3:19; Proverbs 31:10-31; Genesis 2:18-25 as you formulate your articles.

2. NOW, **share** your "ideal husband" assignments with each other, comparing what you have written. Discuss all similarities and differences. What would you add, subtract, change, expand or correct to make what you wrote more Biblical and useful?

3. Each of you complete the **Scorecard For Future Husbands.** (Note that there is one form for the husband-to-be and another for the wife-to-be). Discuss your evaluations with each other.

4. Get together with a Godly, successful husband and interview him about being a husband. Ask him questions such as: What is a Godly husband's responsibilities to his wife? What does the Bible mean when it says that the husband is the head of the wife? What is involved in being the manager of the home? How can you know and fulfill your wife's needs? How can you develop a deep friendship with your wife? How can a husband provide leadership without demeaning or quenching his wife's initiative and creativity? What are the most important factors in being a good husband? How can a husband help her to grow in her God-given potential?

Preparing for Marriage
God's Way

SCORECARD FOR FUTURE HUSBANDS

To be completed by the man

Use this inventory to evaluate yourself as a potential husband. This inventory enumerates issues that are important factors in a good husband/wife relationship. If you are going to be the kind of husband God wants you to be, the factors that will make you that kind of husband will be evident in your life right now. On those statements where you score high (4 or 3), praise God and make sure you keep on doing these things. On those items where your score is 2 or lower, accept the challenge and work on improving.

Rating scale: 0 = never; 1 = rarely; 2 = sometimes; 3 = frequently; 4 = regularly

1. I plan my time so that I can spend time with my partner. 01234

2. I am courteous to her and treat her with respect. 01234

3. I listen to her suggestions, advice and even complaints without ignoring them, being threatened or resenting the fact that she gave them. 01234

4. I communicate with her, telling her what I am doing, where I am going, what my daily schedule involves. 01234

5. I am on time for dates and call her if an emergency arises that will make me late. 01234

6. I help my partner with her responsibilities. 01234

7. I make time for the two of us to be alone together. 01234

8. I refrain from shouting at her, abusing her, talking harshly or unkindly to her or making unreasonable demands on her. 01234

9. I refrain from using force (physical or psychological) to get my own way. 01234

10. I avoid talking to her about women in a way that implies she is inferior. 01234

11. I am willing to work hard enough to adequately provide for household and personal expenses. 01234

12. I work on keeping myself physically attractive. 01234

13. I seek her counsel and advice. 01234

14. I look for positive qualities and behavior and enthusiastically commend her. 01234

15. I show respect and esteem for her when around people; I am courteous and mannerly with her. 01234

16. I avoid being a nitpicker, making mountains out of molehills. 01234

17. I love sharing my ideas, interests and life with her. 01234

18. I listen to her even when she is telling me something in which I am not particularly interested. 01234

19. I am a fun person to be with; I take life and myself seriously, but not too seriously. 01234

20. I try to change any habits that are annoying to her. 01234

21. I try to see things from her perspective and am interested in her viewpoints. 01234

22. I try to love her in the way she wants to be loved. 0 1 2 3 4

23. I exercise spiritual leadership, setting an example of servanthood, leading in devotions, praying regularly for and with her. 0 1 2 3 4

24. I am sensitive to her problems and difficulties and try to be an encouragement to her. 0 1 2 3 4

25. I act like she is the most important person in my life next to the Lord; I treat her like she is really valuable; I communicate appreciation. 0 1 2 3 4

*Go back over this list and make a list of all items that were scored 2, 1 or 0. Pray, think about, discuss, and plan how to make improvements on these items.

SCORECARD FOR FUTURE HUSBANDS

To be completed by the woman

Use this inventory to evaluate your future husband. This inventory enumerates issues that are important in a good husband/wife relationship. Your honest assessment can be a helpful tool in preparing for marriage God's way.

Rating scale: 0 = never; 1 = rarely; 2 = sometimes; 3 = frequently; 4 = regularly

1. He plans his time so that he can spend time with me.   0 1 2 3 4

2. He is courteous to me and treats me with respect.   0 1 2 3 4

3. He listens to my suggestions, advice and even complaints without ignoring them, being threatened or resenting the fact that I gave them.   0 1 2 3 4

4. He communicates with me, telling me what he is doing, where he is going, what his daily schedule involves.   0 1 2 3 4

5. He is on time for dates and calls me if an emergency arises that will make him late.   0 1 2 3 4

6. He helps me with my responsibilities.   0 1 2 3 4

7. He makes time for the two of us to be alone together.   0 1 2 3 4

8. He refrains from shouting at me, abusing me, talking harshly or unkindly to me or making unreasonable demands on me.   0 1 2 3 4

9. He refrains from using force (physical or psychological) to get his own way.   0 1 2 3 4

10. He avoids talking to me about women in a way that implies I am inferior.   0 1 2 3 4

11. He is willing to work hard enough to adequately provide for household and personal expenses.   0 1 2 3 4

12. He works on keeping himself physically attractive.   0 1 2 3 4

13. He seeks my counsel and advice.   0 1 2 3 4

14. He looks for positive qualities and behavior and enthusiastically commends me.   0 1 2 3 4

15. He shows respect and esteem for me when around people; he is courteous and mannerly with me.   0 1 2 3 4

16. He avoids being a nitpicker, making mountains out of molehills.   0 1 2 3 4

17. He loves sharing his ideas, interests and life with me.   0 1 2 3 4

18. He listens to me even when I am telling him something in which he is not particularly interested.   0 1 2 3 4

19. He is a fun person to be with; he takes life and himself seriously, but not too seriously.   0 1 2 3 4

20. He tries to change any habits that are annoying to me.   0 1 2 3 4

21. He tries to see things from my perspective and is interested in my viewpoints.   0 1 2 3 4

22. He tries to love me in the way I want to be loved.   0 1 2 3 4

23. He exercises spiritual leadership, setting an example of servanthood, leading in devotions, praying regularly for and with me.   0 1 2 3 4

24. He is sensitive to my problems and difficulties and tries to be an encouragement to me.   0 1 2 3 4

25. He acts like I am the most important person in his life next to the Lord; he treats me like I am really valuable; he communicates appreciation.   0 1 2 3 4

List items on which you would like to see improvement.

BEING A WIFE GOD'S WAY

God has a plan for husband/wife relationships. It's a good plan because He is a good, merciful and all-wise God. Understanding and following His plan is the pathway to marital bliss and a part of real wisdom. Ignoring or distorting His plan is foolish and disastrous.

In session 9, you learned God's plan for husbands in marriage. Ideally, you were able to come to an agreement on what a husband should be in God's kind of marriage. Similarly, this session on God's plan for wives will help you explore the same mindedness on this important aspect of marriage.

So roll up your sleeves, pray fervently for God's assistance, put on your thinking cap, pick up Bible and pen, find a quiet place and go to work on the following assignments.

1. Each one of you write a **brief article** built on the phrases: "An Ideal Wife is. . ." and "In Marriage, I think the wife should. . ." In the article, be specific, practical, clear, concrete and as thorough as possible. Study Proverbs 31:10-31; Proverbs 18:22; Genesis 2:18-25; Ephesians 5:22-33; I Peter 3:1-8; Titus 2:4, 5 as you write this article.

2. Now, **share** your "ideal wife" assignments with each other. Compare what each of you wrote, and discuss all similarities and differences. What would you add, subtract, change, expand, or correct what you wrote to make it more Biblical and useful?

3. Each of you complete the **Scorecard For Future Wives.** (Note that there is one form for the wife-to-be and another for the husband-to-be.) Discuss your evaluations with each other.

4. Get together with a Godly, successful wife and interview her on what it means to be God's kind of wife. Ask her questions such as: What are the wife's God-given responsibilities to her husband? What does the Bible mean by submission? What does it involve? What does it mean for the wife to be her husband's helper? How can a wife be in submission and yet not stifle or neglect her God-given abilities? How can a wife remind, correct, advise her husband without being bossy or nagging? What are the most important factors in being a Godly wife?

Preparing for Marriage
God's Way

SCORECARD FOR FUTURE WIVES

To be completed by the woman

Use this inventory to evaluate yourself as a potential wife. This inventory enumerates issues that are important factors in a good husband/wife relationship. If you are going to be the kind of wife God wants you to be, the factors that will make you that kind of wife will be evident in your life right now. On those statements where you score high (4 or 3), praise God and make sure you keep on doing these things. On those items where your score is 2 or lower, accept the challenge and work on improving.

Rating scale: 0 = never; 1 = rarely; 2 = sometimes; 3 = frequently; 4 = regularly

1. I take pride in my bedroom, apartment or home by making it attractive and cheerful.   0 1 2 3 4

2. I handle my finances responsibly.   0 1 2 3 4

3. I keep myself attractive in appearance so that my partner is glad to have everyone know that I am the girl he plans to marry.   0 1 2 3 4

4. I am a good sport, cheerful, uncomplaining, appreciative and not a nag.   0 1 2 3 4

5. I am willing to let my partner have his own way and the last word when we disagree.   0 1 2 3 4

6. I avoid making a fuss over minor problems that I should handle alone.   0 1 2 3 4

7. I show respect and admiration for my partner, not comparing him unfavorably with other men, but making him know that I esteem him above all other men.   0 1 2 3 4

8. I show courtesy and consideration to his parents and to his other relatives.   0 1 2 3 4

9. I take a sympathetic and intelligent interest in his work, yet leave him a free hand realizing that he must sometimes give time to his work that we would rather have together.   0 1 2 3 4

10. I cultivate an interest in his friends and recreations so that I can make a satisfactory partner of his leisure hours.   0 1 2 3 4

11. I pray regularly with and for my partner and maintain a good devotional life.   0 1 2 3 4

12. I seek his counsel on important decisions.   0 1 2 3 4

13. I support his decisions and cheerfully assist him in fulfilling them.   0 1 2 3 4

14. I show respect and esteem for him around other people.   0 1 2 3 4

15. I lovingly share my ideas, problems, joys, interests and affection with him on a regular basis.   0 1 2 3 4

16. I avoid shouting and screaming at him.   0 1 2 3 4

17. I refrain from using force or threats or punishment to get my own way.   0 1 2 3 4

18. I avoid allowing my friends or activities to interfere with time to fulfill his desires. 0 1 2 3 4

19. I refrain from embarrassing him or putting him down.   0 1 2 3 4

20. I keep myself internally as well as externally attractive.   0 1 2 3 4

21. I am a "fun person" to be with.   0 1 2 3 4

22. I keep appointments, am on time for dates, call if my plans are changed.   0 1 2 3 4

23. I accept responsibilities, and faithfully fulfill them.   0 1 2 3 4

24. I am sensitive to his problems and difficulties and try to be an encouragement to him.   0 1 2 3 4

25. I try to change habits that are annoying to him.   0 1 2 3 4

    Go back over these questions and note every question you rated 2 or below. The content of these questions will give you ideas on how you can improve. Also, note the questions you answered with a 3 or 4. These are areas where you are doing fine. Keep them in mind so you will continue to do them.

SCORECARD FOR FUTURE WIVES

To be completed by the man

Rating scale: 0 = never; 1 = rarely; 2 = sometimes; 3 = frequently; 4 = regularly

1. She tries to make her apartment or home interesting, attractive and cheerful, devoting as much thought and study to it as she would to a job downtown. 0 1 2 3 4

2. She handles the finances which are her responsibility in a businesslike fashion. 0 1 2 3 4

3. She keeps herself attractive (though not offensively so) so that I am glad to have everyone know that she is to be my wife. 0 1 2 3 4

4. She is a good sport, cheerful, uncomplaining, appreciative and not a nag. 0 1 2 3 4

5. She is willing to let me have my own way and the last word when we disagree. 0 1 2 3 4

6. She avoids making a fuss over trifles and solves minor problems that she should handle alone. 0 1 2 3 4

7. She shows respect and admiration for me, not comparing me unfavorably with other men, but making me think that she esteems me above all other men. 0 1 2 3 4

8. She prevents her mother and other relatives from intruding unduly, and shows courtesy and consideration to my relatives. 0 1 2 3 4

9. She takes a sympathetic and intelligent interest in my work, yet leaves me a free hand realizing that I must sometimes give time to my work that I would rather have with her. 0 1 2 3 4

10. She cultivates an interest in my friends and recreation, so that she can make a satisfactory partner of my leisure hours. 0 1 2 3 4

11. She prays regularly with and for me and maintains a good devotional life. 0 1 2 3 4

12. She seeks my counsel on important decisions. 0 1 2 3 4

13. She supports my decisions and cheerfully assists me in fulfilling them. 0 1 2 3 4

14. She shows respect and esteem for me around other people. 0 1 2 3 4

15. She lovingly shares her ideas, problems, joys, interests and affection on a regular basis. 0 1 2 3 4

16. She avoids shouting and screaming at me. 0 1 2 3 4

17. She refrains from using force or threats or punishing me to get her own way. 0 1 2 3 4

18. She avoids allowing her friends or activities to interfere with time to fulfill my desires. 0 1 2 3 4

19. She refrains from embarrassing me or putting me down. 0 1 2 3 4

20. She keeps herself internally as well as externally attractive. 0 1 2 3 4

21. She is a "fun person" to be with. 0 1 2 3 4

22. She keeps appointments, is on time for dates, calls if plans are changed. 0 1 2 3 4

23. She accepts responsibilities, and faithfully fulfills them. 0 1 2 3 4

24. She is sensitive to my problems and tries to be an encouragement to me.   0 1 2 3 4

25. She tries to change any habits that are annoying to me.   0 1 2 3 4

*List items on which you would like to see improvement.

Session 11:
FAMILY FINANCES GOD'S WAY

"**M**oney isn't everything in life, but it's far ahead of whatever else is in second place." This quip made by who knows who was probably spoken in jest. Unfortunately, it does depict the attitude that many have towards money.

Instinctively we know that there is something wrong with this attitude. Yet, all too often many of us act as if it were true. We behave as if money were the most importnat thing in life, as if our very lives consisted in the abundance of things that we possess. We make decisions based primarily upon the financial rewards we will receive. We think of it, dream of it, work for it, hoard it, waste it, count it and recount it. It becomes a dominant, perhaps *the* dominant theme of our lives.

Others (probably fewer in number) react against this love of money with a disdain for money. They guard against materialism. They believe in the simple lifestyle. They may even make decisions based on their disdain for money. Their motto may be: If it is financially rewarding or costly, it probably is wrong. They may avoid certain things and refuse to purchase certain things, or go to certain places because of the money involved.

Indeed, there are differing opinions about money, and these conflicting views can have a devastating effect on people and relationships. Conflicting ideas about finances are often a part of marital disfunction. In fact, in some cases the major complaint against the other person involves money.

This fact raises a very important question for Christians contemplating marriage: What is God's plan for family finances? What should a Christian's attitude towards money be? How does God want you to handle your finances?

In His Word, God has given clear, solid guidelines and principles for viewing and handling finances. In this session, you will be directed into a practical and highly beneficial study of these principles.

So roll up your sleeves, pray fervently for God's help, find a quiet place, pick up Bible and pen, put on your thinking cap and go to work on the following assignments. Allow God to use His Word to challenge and mold your thoughts in this very important area of your life and relationship. As you explore this subject, let God bring the two of you to same mindedness.

1. Do all the discussion and study questions on the **Handling Family Finances** form.

2. Complete the **Handling Family Finances** form, **Personal Financial Profile** and **Budget For The First Year Of Marriage.** God has called us to be good stewards of all that He has given us. This includes our MONEY. To be a good steward, it is important that we plan and budget to do so.

3. God has not left us alone in this world to fend for ourselves. He has given us His Word and His Spirit to lead and guide us. And,

Preparing for Marriage
God's Way

He has also given us other believers to help us grow more like Jesus. Use this resource that God has given you by discussing with a Godly couple some or all of the questions included in this book. Ask them about financial issues or conflicts that have arisen in their relationship and how they have resolved or are attempting to resolve them. Pick their brains and learn all you can from them that will help you to handle your family finances God's way.

4. If living at home, determine what each of you are costing your parents. Also determine the income and expenditures of each of your families. Identify the possible effects of any differences. If you are not living at home and are supporting yourselves, each of you should fulfill the same assignment with this alteration in mind.

5. Estimate when the greatest periods of financial needs will probably occur and plan how you will prepare for them.

6. Write a brief summary of your response to these assignments; note how they challenged you and helped you, potential problem areas, questions which you would like to ask.

7. If it is appropriate (depending upon the date of your wedding and the laws of your particular state), schedule an appointment to see your physician for a complete physical examination, for birth control information and for a blood test. You will need to have a physical examination and blood test in order to apply for your marriage license.

HANDLING FAMILY FINANCES

1. Discuss and record your personal views about:

   a. The basis on which you will select your occupation and place of employment
   b. credit buying, charge accounts, and loans
   c. savings accounts and investments
   d. giving to the church, needy people, parents, and children
   e. spending money on amusements, entertainment, recreation and vacation
   f. financial planning, budgeting, and bookkeeping
   g. the husband working overtime or having a second job
   h. having a job that requires you to work evenings and be away from home for periods of time
   i. the wife taking a job
   j. financial priorities (furniture or automobile, husband's or wife's clothing, etc.)
   k. insurance
   l. making out a will
   m. providing for emergencies
   n. who will pay the bills and handle routine financial affairs
   o. buying or spending without the other person's agreement
   p. providing for old age
   q. going out to dinner
   r. buying or renting a home
   s. joint or separate bank accounts
   t. spending money on gifts for each other
   u. how much should be spent on clothes, furniture, automobiles, hobbies, etc.

2. Discuss and record the attitudes your respective parents had toward money. Were they savers or spenders? Were they conscientious about paying bills? Did they budget their money? Did they spend money for luxuries or only for necessities? Were they generous in giving to the church and others? Was making money a major focus of their lives? Did they make joint decisions about money? Did your mother have money apportioned to her for spending? Who was in charge of the finances? Did they keep good records? Did your mother work? Did they have joint or separate bank accounts? Did they have a savings account, insurance or investments? Did they buy new automobiles or furniture frequently? Did they frequently repaint or redecorate? Were they self-producers? (Evaluate how your respective parents differed and where your attitudes and financial outlook is like theirs and different from your mate's. Your differing viewpoints may be fertile soil for bitterness, irritation, and resentment unless you can come to a mutually satisfying agreement. Discuss how you can resolve your differences.)

3. List a number of truths about finances found in:

   Psalm 24:1

   _____

   _____

   _____

   1 Chronicles 29:11, 12

   _____

   _____

Proverbs 11:24, 25, 28; 12:10; 13:11; 10:4, 13:18, 24; 15:16, 17, 22; 16:8, 16

_____

_____

_____

1 Thessalonians 4:10-12

_____

_____

_____

Ephesians 4:28

_____

_____

_____

1 Timothy 6:3-10, 17-18

_____

_____

_____

Proverbs 3:9, 10

_____

_____

_____

Luke 14:28

_____

_____

_____

Proverbs 6:6-8

_____

_____

_____

Proverbs 21:5; 16:3

_____

_____

_____

Romans 13:6-8

_____

_____

Proverbs 27:23, 24; 20:18; 19:22

_____

_____

_____

PERSONAL FINANCIAL PROFILE

I. Estimate the value for each item below you own:

ITEM	ESTIMATED VALUE
Home (owned since)	$ _____
Car (number owned)	$ _____
Furnishings	$ _____
Savings	$ _____
Investments	$ _____
Loans due you	$ _____
Collections (stamps, coins)	$ _____
Life insurance	
(cash surrender value)	$ _____
Other Assets	$ _____
_____	$ _____
_____	$ _____

II. List what you currently owe:

ITEM	TOTAL	MONTHLY PAYMENT
Home Mortgage(s)	$ _____	$ _____
Car Loan(s)	$ _____	$ _____
Personal Loan(s)	$ _____	$ _____
Credit Card(s)	$ _____	$ _____
Store Loan(s)	$ _____	$ _____
Other Debts	$ _____	$ _____
_____	$ _____	$ _____
_____	$ _____	$ _____

BUDGET FOR THE FIRST YEAR OF MARRIAGE

Try to complete this form as realistically as possible. Make an educated guess about the items you don't know the exact cost.

Flexible Expenses

Furniture/household equipment/repairs $ _____

Medical and dental care   _____

Vacation and travel (include honeymoon if not paid before wedding)   _____

Christmas, birthdays and other gifts   _____

Education/schooling   _____

Entertainment/hobbies/recreation   _____

Allowances/lunches   _____

Occupational/business expenses   _____

Living Expenses

Food and household supplies   _____

Cleaning and laundry   _____

Personal supplies (cosmetics, haircuts, clothes, etc.)   _____

Newspapers, magazines, books, subscriptions   _____

Transportation

Automobile purchases and/or monthly payments   _____

Automobile operation/maintenance (gas, oil, repairs)   _____

Total Flexible Expenses   _____

Fixed Expenses

Tithes and offerings to the church   _____

Charitable contributions other than the church   _____

Housing (rent or mortgage)   _____

Vehicle licenses and driver's licenses   _____

Professional or union dues   _____

Organizational memberships   _____

Professional journals   _____

Taxes

Property   _____

School   ————

Other assessments   ————

Federal Income Tax   ————

State/local taxes   ————

Utilities

Heat (gas, oil)   ————

Electric   ————

Telephone   ————

Water   ————

Sewer/garbage   ————

Insurance

Automobile   ————

Life   ————

Hospitalization/health/medical   ————

Homeowners/apartment dwellers   ————

Other _____   ————

Installment Payments

Loans (other than automobile or mortgage)   ————

Department stores   ————

Credit cards   ————

Savings/investments   ————

Other debts   ————

Total Fixed Expenses   ————

Summary/Tabulation

Total Flexible Expenses	_____
+ Total Fixed Expenses	_____
= Total Expenses	_____
Income of Husband	_____ (take home)
+ Income of Wife	_____ (take home)
= Total Income	_____
Total Income	_____
− Total Expenses	_____
Difference + or −	_____

If your expenses are greater than your income, check your arithmetic to be sure you added correctly. Also, check each item to confirm that you estimated expenses realistically. If your expenses are greater than your income, discuss how and where you can decrease expenses or increase income.

Session 12:
SEX AS GOD INTENDED

Sex is one of the great gifts God has given to men and women. Within the confines of the marriage relationship, it is intended to be a beautiful expression of unity and oneness. Unfortunately, as you are certainly aware, mankind has perverted this wonderful gift and destroyed the beauty of God's plan.

In our marriage counseling experience, we have become increasingly aware of the heartache that people encounter in marriage because of problems in the area of their sexual relationship. Complaints about sexual disagreements and disappointments seem to be a common factor with many couples, whether they are Christian or not.

Some people see sex relations as the fulcrum of the entire relationship, the most important thing in life. If the bells don't ring and the bands don't constantly play in this area, their marriage and their lives are total disasters. In reality, how things are going in their sexual relationship becomes the measuring stick by which everything in their marriage is evaluated.

On the other hand, there are individuals who consider sexual relationship unpleasant and distasteful. Or they see it as unimportant and unnecessary. Sex relations may be necessary if you want to have children, but beyond that it has no purpose, they believe.

Occasionally, these individuals may be willing to pacify their partner who has a much stronger sexual interest. Personally, however, they would be willing to forego this aspect of marriage almost entirely. Either, they have no desire for sex or they have an intense aversion to it.

This scenario is only one of many that occur in marital conflict in the area of sex relations. The actual particulars of what is involved in sexual conflict may vary in numerous ways. The point is, that whatever those particulars may be, they can be the context in which great marital distress and misery is experienced.

Indeed, exploring this aspect of the marital relationship carefully is no small, insignificant matter. It's a vital part of preparing for marriage God's way.

As you focus on this subject, be open and honest about the items you are going to discuss. If you feel a little embarrassed talking about sexual things with each other or your counselor/teacher, don't back off; ask God for help and press on.

In His Word, God has given much information and many directions about sex relations. And when He does, He doesn't stutter or blush or hide His face. True, He says it discreetly and in a wholesome way. But HE SAYS IT.

Reflect on the fact that if God's Word openly speaks about sex, then it must be all right, even important, for you to reflect on it. It follows also that it must be appropriate (even necessary) for

NOTES

Preparing for Marriage
God's Way

your Godly counselor/teacher to openly yet discreetly discuss a Biblical perspective on sex relations with you.

Please be open and honest with your counselor/teacher about your feelings and thoughts. If you feel embarrassed or think that the issues considered are too personal, share that with your counselor, along with your feelings and thoughts.

So roll up your sleeves, pray for God's help, find a quiet place, pick up Bible and pen, put on your thinking cap and go to work on the following assignments.

1. Complete **The Marriage Act Worksheet.**

2. Complete the questionnaire entitled **Questions For Sexual Discussion.**

3. Write out a **brief summary** of your response to these assignments; how they challenged you and helped you, potential problem areas, and any questions you would like to ask.

Preparing for Marriage
God's Way

THE MARRIAGE ACT WORKSHEET

1. Study I Corinthians 7:2-5; Proverbs 5:15-19; Ephesians 5:22-33 and Genesis 1:27, 28; 2:18-25 and determine several purposes of marriage.

   _____

   _____

   _____

2. Write your own paraphrase of Hebrews 13:4 (you may want to compare a number of translations before you do).

   _____

   _____

   _____

3. List a number of truths about sexual relations found in Proverbs 5:15-21; Song of Solomon 4:1-7; 5:10-16; 7:1-10 and I Corinthians 7:2-5.

   _____

   _____

   _____

4. Study Acts 20:35 and Philippians 2:3-4 and determine how the principles of these verses can be applied to sexual relations.

   _____

   _____

   _____

5. If birth control is a problem for you, study the following verses and see if anything in them is of help in this regard: I Corinthians 7:2-5; Proverbs 5:15-20; I Timothy 5:8; Philippians 2:4; Ephesians 5:25, 28, 29; Exodus 20:13; Genesis 1:27, 28; James 2:17-20; Proverbs 14:15; Proverbs 22:3.

   _____

   _____

   _____

6. As God looked upon Adam and Eve having sexual relations, what do you think was His attitude? What is your attitude as you anticipate sexual relations in marriage? Do you have any fears? What place should sex relations have in a marriage relationship? How often should a couple have sex relations? What should a couple do if they have problems in this area of their marriage?

   _____

   _____

   _____

7. Are the following statements true or false?

    a. Married people should freely tell each other what pleases them in sex relations. T or F

    b. At times it's all right to make excuses to avoid sexual relationships. T or F

    c. Using street language or harsh language is a good practice in reference to sex relations. T or F

    d. Men can enjoy sex more than women. T or F

    e. Strong sexual desire in marriage is a sign of a lack of spirituality. T or F

    f. Married people should freely discuss their sexual relationship with each other. T or F

    g. Married people should be free to tell each other that sex is not appealing to them occasionally. T or F

    h. Since a couple's sexual relationship is a private matter, if problems occur they should not seek help from someone outside the marriage. T or F

    i. Women should not initiate sex relations. T or F

    j. In many cases the biggest hindrance to good sexual relations is a negative attitude. T or F

    k. Whatever is mutually enjoyable and fulfilling to the couple and does not hurt anyone or violate Biblical principle is proper in the confines of a couple's bedroom. T or F

    l. God is pleased when a married couple has sex. T or F

    m. God intended sex to be fun, satisfying and desirable for the husband and wife. T or F

    n. Sexual bargaining is wrong. T or F

    o. Selfishness in sexual relations is forbidden by Scripture. T or F

    p. Selfishness may be manifested in withholding sex or in demanding sex. T or F

    q. Sex relations in marriage are to be regular and continuous. T or F

    r. Abstinence from sexual relationships in marriage is a sign of deep spirituality. T or F

    s. In marriage, every sexual urge should be followed. T or F

    t. Frequency of sex relations should be regulated by the satisfaction principle. T or F

    u. A person shouldn't think about having sex with his spouse. T or F

    v. Intercourse equals sex relations. T or F

    w. Sexual problems (hang-ups) are often symptoms of personal problems or relationship problems. T or F

QUESTIONS FOR SEXUAL DISCUSSION

Write your answers to the following questions individually. Then discuss them with each other. Bring your answers and any additional questions or concerns about sex to the next session, for discussion with your counselor/teacher.

1. Do you recall any specific event or events that have influenced your attitude toward, feelings and thoughts about sex? Explain.

   _____
   _____
   _____
   _____
   _____

2. What was your parents' attitude toward sex?

   _____
   _____
   _____
   _____
   _____

3. What did you learn from your parents about sex either directly or indirectly, verbally or nonverbally?

   _____
   _____
   _____
   _____

4. Did your parents talk freely to you about sex? What did they say? What kind of instruction did they give you?

   _____
   _____
   _____
   _____
   _____

5. Did you talk to your parents about your sexual concerns? Did you ask them questions? If so, what kind of questions? Did they answer these questions with or without embarrassment? Were you satisfied with the answers they gave?

_____

_____

_____

_____

_____

6. Was physical affection shown freely by your parents to one another and to you and your brothers and sisters?

_____

_____

_____

_____

_____

7. Do you recall playing sex games as a child? If so, how did you feel as you were involved in playing these games? Were you discovered playing these games? What happened? What was your reaction to what happened?

_____

_____

_____

_____

8. What stirs up sexual guilt or shame in you now? What embarrasses you about sex?

_____

_____

_____

_____

9. When did you learn where babies come from and how they are conceived? How did you learn? How did you react to this information?

_____

_____

_____

_____

10. As you anticipate marriage, what are your thoughts about sexual intercourse? What are your expectations? What causes some concern or apprehension?

_____

_____

_____

_____

_____

11. Describe your concept of the differences between men and women in the area of sex. Is there any difference? If so, what is it? What roles or activities should the husband perform in sex relations? What roles or activities should the wife perform?

_____

_____

_____

_____

_____

12. What form(s) of contraceptives will you use? Do you and your partner agree? Do you fully understand how the contraceptives you have chosen work? Are you aware of any side effects? How reliable are they?

_____

_____

_____

_____

13. Have you and your partner talked about children? Have you agreed on the number of children you would like to have? When would you like to start a family? Have you agreed on when you want to begin having children? Have you discussed how far apart (time wise) you want to attempt to space your children?

_____

_____

_____

_____

Session 13:
POTPOURRI. WEDDING DETAILS AND SHORTLY THEREAFTER

CONGRATULATIONS! By this time, you have completed twelve sessions designed to prepare you for your upcoming marriage. You've been giving serious attention to preparing for marriage God's way. Surely you've expended effort and have benefited by this endeavor.

Now you have a deeper and broader understanding of God's desires for your marriage. Already you're beginning to reap the results of your faithful efforts. Already, you've been able to apply what you have considered in your life and relationship.

As a result of these studies, one of two things should have occurred. You are either more ready for marriage, or you've come to the conclusion that you are not ready for marriage, at least not right now.

Either way, your efforts have been beneficial. If you've decided that you shouldn't get married right away, your decision has been a painful one. If you're not prepared for marriage God's way, you will be preventing something from occurring that may be even more painful and disastrous. In the long run, that will be beneficial.

Make sure that your concerns and reasons for postponement are justified. Be aware that most people experience some fears and hesitation as the wedding day approaches. It's quite normal to experience some ambivalence! After all, marriage is a serious business. As Christians, it's until death do you part. The privileges and responsibilities are many, and many changes will take place.

However, don't make more out of your fears than you legitimately should. At the same time, if you have good reasons for thinking you are not ready to build your marriage God's way, don't ignore those convictions. As counselors who have seen the devastation caused when unprepared people get married, we commend you for the maturity and honesty to acknowledge it. We also urge you to seek personal help concerning the reasons for your decision.

Most who complete this course have had a different experience. For you, working through *Preparing for Marriage God's Way* has increased your desire and readiness for marriage. Now you're more eager to marry than you were when you began. You see real growth in yourself, your partner and your relationship. You're longing for the time when the two of you will become one as you are joined together in holy wedlock.

If that's the case, let's proceed with the four main purposes for this session.

1. Consolidate and assess what you have accomplished during the last twelve sessions. To facilitate this goal, review the material covered in every previous session. Write down the most important principles from every session. Evaluate how you are

doing in applying these principles. Be ready to share examples of how you are succeeding or failing.

2. Think through and write down issues that you would like to consider in this session. They may be issues that were not discussed to your satisfaction or ones that were not even explored.

3. In this session, you will be finalizing wedding details. Keep in mind that your wedding ceremony is a worship service. It is a worship service in which God's people assemble to thank Him for the gift of marriage and to witness a solemn giving and receiving of vows. It is also a worship service in which the two of you will thank God for each other and covenant yourselves to each other before God for as long as you both shall live. Keep this truth in mind as you plan your special day.

As you prepare for this big day, don't allow the many last-minute wedding details to rob you of the joy and excitement that this day should hold. Remember, the most important thing about the day is not how the flowers look or the color of the brides-maid's dresses. The most important thing about your wedding day is that you will come as *two* and leave as *one*. REJOICE and be exceedingly glad, for God has been good to you!

Be sure to spend time individually and unitedly thinking about what kind of ceremony you want to have. What special music are you going to have? Are you going to write your own vows or do you want to choose prewritten vows? What topic would you like the pastor to focus on during his meditation?

4. The fourth purpose of this session is preparation for a good, beneficial honeymoon. Probably by now, you have planned a lot of the details of your honeymoon. Enjoy the thrill of arranging your first vacation as husband and wife!

In many ways, your honeymoon can be the best vacation of your life. However, for some who were not adequately prepared, it was a very hard experience. Don't let that happen to you. Let your honeymoon be a pleasant experience that you will remember with joy. Plan your honeymoon prayerfully, intelligently, carefully and unitedly. Discuss your honeymoon with your counselor/teacher.

On your honeymoon, don't allow yourself to become so worked up that you forget all that you have learned during these 13 training sessions. Reflect on what you have studied. Rely on the Lord, step out in faith and deal in love with any problems that may arise. Love does cover a multitude of sins (I Peter 4:8). And, if you really get stuck, call your counselor/teacher. Yes, even while you are on your honeymoon! DO NOT LET ANY LITTLE PROBLEMS REMAIN UNSOLVED! Remember, it only takes a little match to start a giant fire.

Preparing for Marriage
God's Way

Session 14:
AFTER THE WEDDING 6 WEEKS' CHECK UP

In preparation for this session, complete these assignments:

1. On the day before this session, fill out the **Rate Your Marriage Inventory** form on the following pages. Circle the numbers representing items that cause you any concern.

2. Make a journal of the high points and low points of your relationship from the wedding until this session. Note any conflicts, problems, annoyances that have arisen and how you handled or resolved them.

3. Keep a family devotional, a spiritual life journal. Note what you have studied together, how your corporate prayer life is going, difficulties you have faced in this area, how you have helped and are helping one another to grow spiritually, as well as any questions or concerns you may have.

4. Write down any issues or questions you want to discuss with your counselor/teacher and bring them with you to the next session.

Preparing for Marriage
God's Way

RATE YOUR MARRIAGE INVENTORY

Name _____ **Date** _____

This inventory is designed to evaluate how you are doing in your marriage relationship and to spot problem areas so that you may work on correcting them. The inventory will be most beneficial if you will take it individually and then sit down and discuss your respective answers to each question. Seek to understand clearly your mate's reasons for giving the rating that he/she did. If your ratings pinpoint some difficulties, focus on how to resolve problems. Don't just attack or blame your mate. It will be of no benefit for you to defend yourself. Remember, God does have a solution to every problem if you will only handle your problems and seek to solve them in a Biblical way. View and use this inventory in a constructive way.

Rating scale: Always = 4; Often/frequently = 3; Sometimes = 2; Seldom = 1; Never = 0. Write the number that describes what you judge to be true of your marriage in the blank following each question.

1. Does the fact that Jesus Christ is Lord manifest itself in practical ways in your marriage? _____

2. Do you use the Bible to determine your convictions, decisions and practices in life in general and marriage in particular? _____

3. Do you and your spouse study the Bible and pray together? _____

4. Do you worship God together with other believers? _____

5. Do you serve God together in activities that will build up the church and honor Christ? _____

6. Do you and your spouse seek to please one another? _____

7. Do you ask for forgiveness when you have done something wrong? _____

8. Do you take full responsibility for your thoughts, actions and reactions? _____

9. Do you allow your mate to disagree with you without becoming nasty or punishing him/her? _____

10. Do you allow your spouse to make mistakes without becoming nasty or punishing him/her? _____

11. Do you focus on the things that are commendable, praiseworthy and good about your mate? _____

12. Do you express appreciation to your mate in tangible ways? Do you express gratitude and thanks? _____

13. Do you communicate in an in-depth way with each other daily? _____

14. Do you express your opinions, ideas, plans, aspirations, fears, feelings, likes, dislikes, views, problems, joys, frustrations and annoyances to each other? _____

15. Do you and your mate understand each other when you try to express yourselves? _____

16. Do you do many different things together and enjoy being with each other? Are you involved in common projects? _____

17. Do you show love in many practical and tangible ways? _____

18. Do you still court one another by occasional gifts, unexpected attention, etc.? _____

19. Is your conversation pleasant and friendly? _____

20. Do you pray for one another, support and seek to encourage one another? _____

21. Can you discuss differing viewpoints on values, priorities, religious convictions, politics, etc. without becoming irritated? _____

22. Do you anticipate sexual relations with your partner? _____

23. Are your sexual desires compatible? _____

24. Do you freely discuss your sexual desires with your mate? _____

25. Do you agree about the way money should be spent? _____

26. Do you think your spouse is as concerned about your views about the way money should be spent as he/she is about his/her own? _____

27. Do you agree on how to bring up children? _____

28. Do you refuse to lie to your spouse; are you building your relationship on speaking the truth? Can your spouse put full confidence in whatever you say, knowing that you really mean what you say? _____

29. Do you have a good relationship with your in-laws? Do you appreciate them? _____

30. Do you really respect your spouse? _____

31. Are you glad to introduce your spouse to friends and associates? _____

32. Do you control yourself when you are moody so that you do not disrupt your relationship and inflict your moodiness on others? _____

33. Do you seek to change your specific habits that may cause discomfort or displeasure to your spouse? _____

34. Do you make your relationship with your spouse a priority matter? _____

35. Do you treat your mate with respect and dignity? _____

36. Do you accept corrective criticisms graciously? _____

37. Do you agree concerning the roles and responsibilities of husband and wife? _____

38. Are you willing to face, discuss and look for Scriptural solutions to problems without blowing up or attacking your mate or dissolving into tears? _____

39. Do you maintain your own spiritual life through Bible reading, prayer, regular church attendance and fellowship with God's people? _____

TOTAL: _____

*Put a circle around the number of any of the previous items that give you any concern about your relationship.

Session 15:
AFTER THE WEDDING 6 MONTHS' CHECK UP

In preparation for this session, complete these assignments:

1. Do the **Ways to Express Love** studies (one for husband and one for wife) in this manual.

2. Choose a two week period in which you will keep a good times/bad times journal.

3. Carefully read and discuss the 34 items on the **Parenting Inventory** in this workbook. Identify for learning, not condemning purposes, how you perceive your family of origin functioned on each of these items. Discuss the possible impact on your own parenting.

4. A day or two before this session, fill out the **Rate Your Marriage Inventory** in this manual. Follow the same procedure for **Communication Test #1** and **#2.**

5. Write down any issues or questions you want to discuss with your counselor/teacher and bring them with you to the next session.

Preparing for Marriage
God's Way

WAYS A HUSBAND MAY EXPRESS LOVE TO HIS WIFE
(How to convince your wife you love her)

The following list sets forth practical ways a husband may express his love to his wife. Use it as a guide to help you evaluate the way you express love to your wife. Circle any ideas you are neglecting which show your wife you love her. Ask her to go over the list and put a check mark in front of the ways she would like you to express love, and to add other things to the list.

You may express love to your wife by:

1. Functioning as the loving leader of your home.

2. Telling her frequently that you love her.

3. Giving her a regular amount of money to spend in any way she chooses.

4. Leading family devotions regularly.

5. Smiling and being cheerful when you come home from work.

6. Helping her wash and dry the dishes or doing them yourself so that she might have time for herself to relax (at least twice a week).

7. Taking her out to dinner or to do some fun thing at least once a week.

8. Doing "fix-it" jobs she wants done around the house (when she wants them done).

9. Greeting her when you come home with a smile, a hug, a kiss and an "Am I glad to see you. I really missed you today." (If she works and comes home after you, then greet her in the same way when she returns home.)

10. Giving her a lingering kiss.

11. Patting her on the shoulder or some other region of her anatomy; holding her hand or caressing her frequently.

12. Being willing to talk to her about her concerns and not belittling her for having those concerns.

13. Looking at her with an adoring expression.

14. Sitting close to her.

15. Rubbing her back or. . .

16. Shaving or taking a bath or brushing your teeth before you have sex relations.

17. Wearing her favorite aftershave lotion.

18. Writing love notes or letters to her.

19. Letting her know that you appreciate her and what you appreciate about her. Do this often and for things that are sometimes taken for granted. Pretend you are trying to convince her you think she is great and very important to you.

20. Fulfilling her implied or unspoken desires or wishes, as well as the specific requests she makes of you. Anticipate what she might desire and surprise her by doing it before she asks.

21. Playing with her; sharing her hobbies and recreational preferences enthusiastically; including her in yours.

22. Seeking to set a good example.

23. Talking about her favorably to others when she can hear you and when she can not.

24. Bragging about her good points as a wife and in every other area to others; letting her know that you are proud to have her as your wife.

25. Maintaining your own spiritual life through Bible study, prayer, regular church attendance and fellowship with God's people.

26. Handling your affairs decently and in order; structuring your time and using it wisely.

27. Making plans prayerfully and carefully.

28. Asking her advice when you have problems or decisions to make.

29. Following her advice unless to do so would violate Biblical principles.

30. Fulfilling your responsibilities.

31. Being sober, but not sombre about life.

32. Having a realistic, Biblical, positive attitude toward life.

33. Discussing plans with your wife before you make decisions, and when the plans are made, sharing them fully with her, giving reasons for making the decisions you did.

34. Thanking her in creative ways for her attempts to please you.

35. Actually changing where and when you should.

36. Sharing your insights, reading, good experiences with her.

37. Planning for a mini-honeymoon where the two of you can do whatever you want to do.

38. Giving a low whistle or some other expression of admiration when she wears a new dress or your favorite negligee or. . .

39. Gently brushing her leg under the table.

40. Being reasonably happy to go shopping with her.

41. Relating what happened at work or whatever you did apart from her.

42. Reminiscing about the early days of your courtship.

43. Expressing appreciation for her parents and relatives.

44. Taking her out to breakfast.

45. Agreeing with her about getting a new dress or some other item.

46. Thanking her when she supports your decisions and cooperates enthusiastically. Especially make it a matter of celebration when she supports and helps enthusiastically at times when you know that she doesn't fully agree.

47. Asking her to have sexual relations with you and seeking to be especially solicitous of her desires. Express gratitude when she tries to please you.

48. Buying gifts for her.

49. Watching her television programs or going where she wants to go instead of watching or doing what you want. Do it cheerfully and enthusiastically.

50. Being cooperative and appreciative when she holds, caresses or kisses you.

51. Running errands gladly.

52. Pampering and making a fuss over her.

53. Being willing to see things from her point of view.

54. Being lovingly honest with her—no backdoor messages—no withholding of the truth that may hinder your present or future relationship.

55. Indicating you want to be alone with her to talk to just lie in each other's arms.

56. Refusing to "cop-out," "blow up," attack, blameshift, withdraw or exaggerate when she seeks to make constructive suggestions or discuss problems.

57. Giving her your undivided attention when she wants to talk.

58. Cheerfully staying up until _____ o'clock to solve a problem or share her burdens.

59. Holding her close while expressing tangible and vocal love when she is hurt, discouraged, weary or burdened.

60. Planning vacations and trips with her.

61. Being eager to share a good joke or some other interesting information you have learned.

62. Going with her in a team ministry in the church.

63. Going to a Bible study or research project together.

64. Establishing and following a family budget.

65. Keeping yourself attractive and neat.

66. Being cooperative, helpful, functioning as a cohost when you have people in for dinner or fellowship.

67. Asking her to pray with you about something.

68. Acknowledging that there are some specific areas or ways in which you need to improve.

69. Refusing to disagree with her in the presence of others.

70. Cooperating with her in establishing family goals and then in fulfilling them.

71. Being available and eager to fulfill her desires whenever and wherever possible and proper.

72. Beginning each day with cheerfulness and tangible expressions of affection.

73. Planning to spend some time alone with her each day for sharing and communicating.

74. Remembering to tell her when you must work late.

75. Refusing to work late on a regular basis.

76. Taking care of the yardwork properly.

77. Refusing to compare her unfavorably with other people.

78. Handling money wisely.

79. Not allowing work, church or recreational activities to keep you from fulfilling marriage responsibilities.

80. Trying to find things to do with her.

81. Being willing to go out or stay home with her.

82. Being polite and courteous and mannerly with her.

83. Refusing to be overly dependent on your parents or friends.

84. Developing mutual friends.

85. Providing hospitalization insurance.

86. Trying to the level of your ability to provide housing and some support for your family in case you should die or become handicapped.

WAYS A WIFE MAY EXPRESS LOVE TO HER HUSBAND
(How to convince your husband you love him)

The following list sets forth practical ways a wife may express her love to her husband. Use it as a guide to help you evaluate the way you express love to your husband. Circle any ideas you are neglecting which show your husband you love him. Ask him to go over the list and put a check mark in front of the ways he would like you to express love, and to add other things to the list.

You may express love to your husband by:

1. Greeting him at the door when he comes home with a smile, a hug, a kiss and an "Am I glad to see you. I really missed you today."

2. Having a cup of coffee or tea (or his favorite beverage) ready for him when he comes home from work.

3. Giving him a lingering kiss.

4. Letting him know you like to be with him and making arrangements so you can spend time with him without giving the impression that you really should or would rather be doing something else.

5. Being willing to talk with him about his concerns and not belittling him for having those concerns.

6. Supporting him and cooperating with him enthusiastically and positively when he has made a decision.

7. Teasing him and flirting with him.

8. Seeking to arouse him and by sometimes being the aggressor or leader in sex relations.

9. Asking him to have sex relations more than he would expect you to.

10. Letting yourself go when having sexual relations.

11. Caressing him.

12. Looking at him with an adoring expression.

13. Holding his hand.

14. Sitting close to him.

15. Rubbing his back or. . .

16. Wearing his favorite nightgown or dress or perfume or. . .

17. Expressing your love in words or notes.

18. Letting him know that you appreciate him and what you appreciate about him. Do this often and for things that are sometimes taken for granted. Pretend you are trying to convince him you think he is great and very important to you.

19. Standing with him and supporting him in his attempt to live for God.

20. Fulfilling his implied or unspoken desires or wishes, as well as the specific requests he makes of you. Anticipate what he might desire and surprise him by doing it before he asks.

21. Playing with him (tennis, golf, party games, etc.); sharing his hobbies and recreational preferences enthusiastically; including him in yours.

22. Enthusiastically cooperating with him and sharing with him in devotions and prayer.

23. Maintaining your own spiritual life through Bible study, prayer, regular church attendance and fellowship with God's people.

24. Handling your affairs decently and in order; structuring your time and using it wisely.

25. Being willing to face and solve problems even if it requires discomfort, change and much effort.

26. Fulfilling your responsibilities.

27. Asking his advice when you have problems or decisions to make.

28. Following his advice unless to do so would violate Biblical principles.

29. Being ready to leave at the appointed time.

30. Thanking him in creative ways for his attempts to please you.

31. Asking for forgiveness and saying, "I was wrong and will try to change."

32. Actually changing where you should.

33. Working with him on his projects or. . .

34. Reading the literature he asks you to read and sharing your insights.

35. Letting him know when he has tough decisions to make, and even when they are not so tough, that you really believe he will choose the right thing and that you will wholeheartedly support him in whatever decision he makes, provided the decision does not violate clearly revealed Biblical principles. Be his best cheerleader and fan club.

36. Buying gifts for him. . .

37. Watching football or some other sporting events with him and trying to really manifest an interest.

38. Cooking creatively and faithfully.

39. Keeping the house neat and clean.

40. Being appreciative and cooperative when he holds you, caresses or kisses you.

41. Lovingly giving him your input when you think he is in error.

42. Offering constructive suggestions when you think he could improve or become more productive. Don't push or preach or do this in such a way that you belittle him, but seek positive and nonthreatening ways to help him become more fully the man God wants him to be.

43. Running errands gladly.

44. Seeking to complete, not compete with him. Be the best member of his team and seek to convince him that you are just that.

45. Being lovingly honest with him—no backdoor messages—no withholding of the truth that may hinder your present or future relationship.

46. Being willing to see things from his point of view; by putting the best interpretation on what he does or says until you have proof that proves the contrary.

47. Pampering him and making a fuss over him.

48. Being happy and cheerful.

49. Refusing to nag.

50. Giving a gentle brush of a leg under the table.

51. Having candlelight and music at dinner.

52. Indicating you want to be alone with him to talk or just lie in each other's arms.

53. Giving an "I promise you" wink.

54. Going for a walk with him.

55. Letting him know you are lonely when he is out of town or away from you for a period of time.

56. Relating what happened to you during your day.

57. Sharing your fears, concerns, joys, failures, etc.

58. Seeking to support your ideas with Biblical insights and good reasons.

59. Refusing to "cop-out," "blow up," attack, blameshift, withdraw or exaggerate when he seeks to make constructive suggestions or discuss problems.

60. Giving him your undivided attention when he wants to talk.

61. Discussing the meaning of certain Bible passages.

62. Cheerfully staying up until _____ o'clock to solve a problem or share his burdens.

63. Holding him close while expressing genuine concern and tangible and vocal love when he is hurt, discouraged, weary or burdened.

64. Being eager to share a good joke or some other interesting information you have learned.

65. Working in the yard, painting a room, washing the car, etc. together.

66. Planning vacations and trips together.

67. Wanting to keep family memorabilia, newspaper clippings, church releases, etc. that have to do with your husband.

68. Bragging about him, his accomplishments and how good a husband he is to other people.

69. Joining him in a team ministry at the church.

70. Doing a Bible study or a Bible research project together.

71. Doing a good job in bookkeeping family finances.

72. Helping prepare the income tax report.

73. Keeping in touch through letters with your family and friends.

74. Keeping yourself attractive and neat.

75. Inviting other people in for dinner and fellowship.

76. Developing and using the spiritual gifts God has given you.

77. Asking him to pray with you about something specific.

78. Managing to stay within the family budget and even save some for special surprises.

79. Being excited about sharing the gospel with others, about answered prayer or helping other people.

80. Making a list for him of things that need to be done around the house.

81. Being satisfied with your present standard of living, furniture or equipment when he can provide no more.

82. Not making nostalgic comments about your father's way of doing things, which may seem to imply that you think your father was a much better man than your husband.

83. Acknowledging that there are some specific areas or ways in which you need to improve.

84. Taking care of his clothes so that he is always well dressed.

85. Appreciating and helping his mother, father and relatives.

86. Refusing to disagree with him or confront him in the presence of others.

87. Cooperating with him in establishing family goals and procedures, and then fulfilling them.

88. Being silly and unconventional at times in your lovemaking.

PARENTING INVENTORY

Study the following principles and rate yourself and your mate on each item:

1 = Excellent; 2 = Good; 3 = Fair; 4 = Poor; 5 = Terrible

	YOU	MATE
1. My expectations for my child are realistic. I have evaluated them in light of the Bible. (1 Corinthians 13:11; Matthew 18:10; Genesis 33:12-14)	____	____
2. I love my child unconditionally. (Genesis 7:7; 1 John 4:10, 19)	____	____
3. I look for opportunities when I can commend my child. I express appreciation for him/her frequently. (Philippians 1:3; 1 Thessalonians 1:2; 2 Thessalonians 1:3)	____	____
4. I seldom criticize without first expressing appreciation for good points.	____	____
5. I give him/her freedom to make decisions where serious issues are not at stake. My goal is to bring my child to maturity in Christ and not dependence upon me. (Proverbs 22:6; Ephesians 4:13-15; 6:4; Colossians 1:27, 28)	____	____
6. I refuse to compare him/her with others. (Galatians 6:4; 2 Corinthians 1:12, 13; 1 Corinthians 12:4-11)	____	____
7. I don't mock or make fun of him/her. I don't demean or belittle my child. I don't call him/her dumb, clumsy or stupid. (Proverbs 12:18; 16:24; Matthew 7:12; Ephesians 4:29, 30; Colossians 4:6)	____	____
8. I don't scold him/her in front of others. (Matthew 16:22, 23; 18:15; 1 Corinthians 16:14)	____	____
9. I don't make threats or promises that I don't intend to keep. (Matthew 5:37; Colossians 3:9; James 5:12)	____	____
10. I am not afraid to say "no" and when I say it, I mean it. (Genesis 18:19; 1 Samuel 3:13; Proverbs 22:15; 29:18)	____	____
11. When my child has problems or is a problem, I do not overreact or lose control of myself. I do not yell, shout or scream at him. (1 Corinthians 16:14; Ephesians 4:26, 27; 1 Timothy 5:1, 2; 2 Timothy 2:24, 25)	____	____
12. I communicate optimism and expectancy. I do not communicate by word or action that I have given up on my child or am resigned to his/her failure. (1 Corinthians 13:7; 2 Corinthians 9:1, 2; Philemon 21)	____	____
13. I am sure that my child knows exactly what is expected of him/her.	____	____
14. I ask his/her advice and include him/her in some of the family planning. (John 6:6; Romans 1:11, 12; 1 Timothy 4:12; 2 Timothy 4:11)	____	____
15. When I make a mistake with my child, I admit it and ask for his/her forgiveness. (Matthew 5:23, 24; James 5:16)	____	____

16. I have family conferences when I discuss family goals, projects, vacations, devotions, chores, disciplines, complaints, suggestions, and problems.

17. I welcome contributions from my child. (Psalms 128; Proverbs 15:22; Titus 1:6-8; James 3:13-18)

18. I assess his/her areas of strength and then encourage him/her to develop them. (2 Timothy 1:16; 4:5, 1 Peter 4:10)

19. I give him/her plenty of tender loving care. I am free in my expression of love by word and deed. (John 13:34; 1 Corinthians 13:1-8; 16:14; 1 Thessalonians 2:7, 8)

20. I practice selective reinforcement. When my child does something well, I commend him/her. I especially communicate when his/her attitudes are what they should be. (Ephesians 1:15; Philemon 1:3-5; Colossians 1:3, 4; 1 Thessalonians 1:3-10)

21. I am more concerned about Christian attitudes and character than I am about performance, athletic skills, clothing, external beauty or intelligence. (1 Samuel 16:7; Proverbs 4:23; Matthew 23:25-28; Galatians 5:22, 23; 1 Peter 3:4, 5)

22. I have a lot of fun with my child. I plan to have many fun times and many special events with my child. I have a list of fun things my family can do. (Psalms 128; Proverbs 5:15-18; 15:13; 17:22; Ecclesiastes 3:4; Ephesians 6:4; Colossians 3:21)

23. I help my child learn responsibility by administering discipline fairly consistently, lovingly and promptly. (1 Samuel 3:13; Proverbs 13:24; 19:18; 2:15)

24. I look upon my child as a human becoming as well as a human being. I look upon the task of raising children as a process which takes years to complete. (Proverbs 22:6; Isaiah 28:9, 10; Galatians 6:9; Ephesians 6:4; 1 Corinthians 15:58)

25. I live my convictions consistently. My child can learn by observing my example as well as by listening to my words. (Deuteronomy 6:4-9; Philemon 4:9; 1 Thessalonians 2:10-12; 2 Timothy 1:5, 7)

26. I recognize that I am responsible to prepare my child for life in this world and in the world to come. (Deuteronomy 6:4-9; Psalms 78:5-7; Ephesians 6:4; 2 Timothy 3:15-17)

27. I am sensitive to the needs, feelings, fears and opinions of my child. (Matthew 18:10; Colossians 3:21)

28. I treat my child as though he is respected by me. (Matthew 18:5, 6)

29. I avoid the use of angry or exasperated words. (Proverbs 15:1; Ephesians 4:31, 32)

30. I maintain the practice of daily Bible reading, discussions, and prayer. (Deuteronomy 6:4-9; Psalms 1:1-3; 78:5-8; 119:9, 11; Ephesians 6:4; 2 Timothy 3:15) _____ _____

31. I am thoroughly involved in a Biblical church. (Ephesians 4:11-16; Hebrews 10:24, 25) _____ _____

32. I make my home a center of Christian hospitality where my child will be brought into frequent contact with many Christians. (2 Kings 4:8-37; Romans 12:13; Hebrews 13:1, 2) _____ _____

33. I make it easy for my child to approach me with problems, difficulties and concerns. I am a good listener when he needs me. I give my child my undivided attention. I avoid being a mind reader, an interrupter or a critic. I show an interest in whatever interests my child. I make myself available when my child needs me—even if I am busy. (1 Corinthians 9:19-23; Philemon 2:3, 4; James 1:19, 20; 3:16-18; 1 John 3:16-18) _____ _____

34. I seek to bring my child to a saving knowledge of Jesus Christ. I become all things to my child that I might win him/her to and for Christ. God, of course, must do the saving, bring conviction, give repentance and faith. I recognize that I may provide the environment in which God saves by my prayers, Godly speech and example, family devotions and involvement in a sound, Biblical church. (Deuteronomy 6:4-9; Mark 10:13, 14; Romans 10:13-17; 3:1; 1 Corinthians 1:18-21; Ephesians 6:4; 2 Timothy 1:5-7; 3:14-17) _____ _____

RATE YOUR MARRIAGE INVENTORY

Name _____ **Date** _____

This inventory is designed to evaluate how you are doing in your marriage relationship and to spot problem areas so that you may work on correcting them. The inventory will be most beneficial if you will take it individually and then discuss your respective answers to each question. Seek to understand clearly the other person's reasons for giving the rating that he/she did. If your ratings pinpoint some difficulties, focus on how to resolve problems. Don't just attack or blame the other person. It will be of no benefit for you to defend yourself. Remember, God does have a solution to every problem if you will only handle your problems and seek to solve them in a Biblical way. View and use this inventory in a constructive way.

Rating scale: Always = 4; Often/frequently = 3; Sometimes = 2; Seldom = 1; Never = 0. Write the number that describes what you judge to be true of your marriage in the blank following each question.

1. Does the fact that Jesus Christ is Lord manifest itself in practical ways in your marriage? _____

2. Do you use the Bible to determine your convictions, decisions and practices in life in general and marriage in particular? _____

3. Do you and your spouse study the Bible and pray together? _____

4. Do you worship God together with other believers? _____

5. Do you serve God together in activities that will build up the church and honor Christ? _____

6. Do you and your spouse seek to please one another? _____

7. Do you ask for forgiveness when you have done something wrong? _____

8. Do you take full responsibility for your thoughts, actions and reactions? _____

9. Do you allow your mate to disagree with you without becoming nasty or punishing him/her? _____

10. Do you allow your spouse to make mistakes without becoming nasty or punishing him/her? _____

11. Do you focus on the things that are commendable, praiseworthy and good about your mate? _____

12. Do you express appreciation to your mate in tangible ways? Do you express gratitude and thanks? _____

13. Do you communicate daily with each other in an in-depth way? _____

14. Do you express your opinions, ideas, plans, aspirations, fears, feelings, likes, dislikes, views, problems, joys, frustrations and annoyances to each other? _____

15. Do you and your mate understand each other when you try to express yourselves? _____

16. Do you do many different things together and enjoy being with each other? Are you involved in common projects? _____

17. Do you show love in many practical and tangible ways?   ———

18. Do you still court one another by occasional gifts, unexpected attention, etc.?   ———

19. Is your conversation pleasant and friendly?   ———

20. Do you pray for one another, support and seek to encourage one another?   ———

21. Can you discuss differing viewpoints on values, priorities, religious convictions,
    politics, etc. without becoming irritated?   ———

22. Do you anticipate sexual relations with your partner?   ———

23. Are your sexual desires compatible?   ———

24. Do you freely discuss your sexual desires with your mate?   ———

25. Do you agree about the way money should be spent?   ———

26. Do you think your spouse is as concerned about your views about the way
    money should be spent as he/she is about his/her own?   ———

27. Do you agree on how to bring up children?   ———

28. Do you refuse to lie to your spouse; are you building your relationship on
    speaking the truth? Can your spouse put full confidence in whatever you say,
    knowing that you really mean what you say?   ———

29. Do you have a good relationship with your in-laws? Do you appreciate them?   ———

30. Do you really respect your spouse?   ———

31. Do you control yourself when you are moody so that you do not disrupt your
    relationship and inflict your moodiness on others?   ———

33. Do you seek to change your specific habits that may cause discomfort or
    displeasure to your spouse?   ———

34. Do you make your relationship with your spouse a priority matter?   ———

35. Do you treat your mate with respect and dignity?   ———

36. Do you accept corrective criticisms graciously?   ———

37. Do you agree concerning the roles and responsibilities of husband and wife?   ———

38. Are you willing to face, discuss and look for Scriptural solutions to problems
    without blowing up or attacking the other person or dissolving into tears?   ———

39. Do you maintain your own spiritual life through Bible reading, prayer, regular
    church attendance and fellowship with God's people?   ———

                                                                            TOTAL: ———

*Put a circle around the number of any of the previous items that give you any concern about your
relationship.

COMMUNICATION TEST #1

This test is based on the principles for good communication as given by the Apostle Paul in Ephesians 4:25-32. Rate yourself and your mate on each category. Discuss your ratings and the reasons for them with each other. Seek to improve all ratings of 3 or higher.

1 = Never; 2 = Rarely; 3 = Sometimes; 4 = Frequently; 5 = Regularly

HINDRANCES TO GOOD COMMUNICATION

	YOU	MATE
1. Deliberate untruth	_____	_____
2. Exaggeration	_____	_____
3. Misrepresentation	_____	_____
4. Promise Breaking	_____	_____
5. Exploding, shouting	_____	_____
6. Silence, withdrawal, retreating, tears	_____	_____
7. Abusive speech	_____	_____
8. Gossip	_____	_____
9. Complaining, grumbling	_____	_____
10. Quarrelsome speech	_____	_____
11. Defensive speech, excuse making, blame shifting	_____	_____
12. Self-centered, boastful speech	_____	_____
13. Hasty, presumptuous, know-it-all speech	_____	_____
14. Nitpicking, fault-finding speech	_____	_____
15. Constant, backdoor messages	_____	_____

COMMUNICATION TEST #2

Rate yourself and your mate on each category. Discuss your ratings and the reasons for them with each other. Seek to improve all ratings of 3 or lower.

1 = Never; 2 = Rarely; 3 = Sometimes; 4 = Frequently; 5 = Regularly

COMMUNICATION PROMPTERS

	YOU	MATE
1. Nonverbal communication regularly (touch, hugs, smiles, etc.)	_____	_____
2. Sharing time daily	_____	_____
3. Fun time weekly (recreation, common interests, lots of laughs)	_____	_____
4. Daily dealing with and resolving conflicts	_____	_____
5. Quick to ask for forgiveness	_____	_____
6. Genuine concern	_____	_____
7. Quick to grant forgiveness	_____	_____
8. Constructive speech	_____	_____
9. Use of first person personal pronouns (singular) when dealing with problems and conflicts	_____	_____
10. Properly timed speech	_____	_____
11. Truthfulness (honesty, makes sure of facts)	_____	_____
12. Allows for differences	_____	_____
13. Careful listening (without interruption, undivided attention, makes sure really understands mate).	_____	_____
14. Expresses praise, appreciation, compliments, respect	_____	_____
15. Gives encouragement when discouraged	_____	_____
16. Expresses interest in mate's personal projects, hobbies, etc.	_____	_____
17. Communicates love in the primary love language of mate.	_____	_____

Session 16:
AFTER THE WEDDING ONE YEAR CHECK UP

In preparation for this session, complete the following assignments. Many of these assignments will take a good deal of time to accomplish and will need to be started several days or weeks before your class session. Therefore, use them as part of your devotions and work on them on a regular basis. Don't wait until a few days before the session to get started.

1. Plan a fun day on which you will do something mutually enjoyable at least once a month. Keep a record of what you do and how you enjoyed or didn't enjoy it.

2. During the month preceding this session, do the **How To Turn One Plus One Into One** study in this manual.

3. During the week before this session, you and your mate each fill out the **Common Interests And Activities** form reflecting what is happening now in your relationship. Each of you specify whether you are satisfied or unsatisfied with the common interests you have.

4. During the week before this session, each of you take **Communication Test #1** and **#2** reflecting what is now happening in this area in your relationship.

5. During the week preceding this session, each of you will fill out the **Rate Your Marriage Inventory.** After taking this evaluative test, circle the numbers of the items that are of any concern for you. You've taken this test on two other occasions, but it serves as a constant means of evaluation concerning your relationship. (Suggestion—use it as a self-evaluative tool for the rest of your life.)

6. During the week before this session, complete the assignments labeled **Personal Inventory #1** and **#2.**

7. Write down any issues you want to discuss. If problems arise you are not able to resolve, call your counselor/teacher before they multiply or intensify.

Preparing for Marriage God's Way

HOW TO TURN ONE PLUS ONE INTO ONE

Instructions: Write out your answers individually. Then get together with your mate, share and discuss them. Agree on any action you want to take as a result of your sharing.

1. When the Bible speaks of marriage as a one-flesh relationship, I think it means. . .

   _____
   _____
   _____

2. When I think of oneness in marriage, I think of. . .

   _____
   _____
   _____

3. In our marriage, I have felt distanced from you when. . .

   _____
   _____
   _____

4. Sometimes it is hard for us to achieve intimacy because. . . _____

   _____
   _____

5. Our oneness could be further enhanced by. . .

   _____
   _____

6. In our relationship I have felt very close to you when. . .

   _____
   _____
   _____

7. We are developing oneness in our relationship by. . .

   _____
   _____
   _____

8. Our oneness in marriage has been, or is being, hindered by. . .

_____

_____

_____

9. Some of the happiest moments I have in our relationship are. . .

_____

_____

_____

10. Three words I would use to describe our relationship are. . .

_____

11. Before either of us dies, I would like to see the following desires for our marriage fulfilled. . .

_____

_____

_____

12. On the day of our wedding, my thoughts and feelings about you were. . .

_____

_____

_____

COMMON INTERESTS AND ACTIVITIES

How do you and your mate participate in the following activities? Check the appropriate space for each item. Let this inventory challenge you if you need to be challenged in terms of common interests.

	Together	Both but not together	One exclusively	One primarily	Neither
Church (attendance and service)	_____	_____	_____	_____	_____
Reading	_____	_____	_____	_____	_____
Competitive Sports (tennis, volleyball. .)	_____	_____	_____	_____	_____
Noncompetitive Sports (jogging, swimming. . .)	_____	_____	_____	_____	_____
Spectator Sports	_____	_____	_____	_____	_____
Outdoor Activities	_____	_____	_____	_____	_____
Social Gatherings (family, friends, church, community. . .)	_____	_____	_____	_____	_____
Clubs, organizations	_____	_____	_____	_____	_____
Art appreciation (listening to music, visiting museum. . .)	_____	_____	_____	_____	_____
Creative and interpretive art (writing, painting)	_____	_____	_____	_____	_____
Hobbies (collecting, gardening, sewing. . .)	_____	_____	_____	_____	_____
Business and professional activities	_____	_____	_____	_____	_____
School functions or organizations	_____	_____	_____	_____	_____
Politics	_____	_____	_____	_____	_____
Motion Pictures	_____	_____	_____	_____	_____
Devotions	_____	_____	_____	_____	_____
Shopping	_____	_____	_____	_____	_____
Table Games	_____	_____	_____	_____	_____
Sightseeing	_____	_____	_____	_____	_____
Entertaining Friends	_____	_____	_____	_____	_____
Other _____	_____	_____	_____	_____	_____

COMMUNICATION TEST #1

This test is based on the principles for good communication as given by the Apostle Paul in Ephesians 4:25-32. Rate yourself and your mate on each category. Discuss your ratings and the reasons for them with each other. Seek to improve all ratings of 3 or higher.

1 = Never; 2 = Rarely; 3 = Sometimes; 4 = Frequently; 5 = Regularly

HINDRANCES TO GOOD COMMUNICATION

	YOU	MATE
1. Deliberate untruth	——	——
2. Exaggeration	——	——
3. Misrepresentation	——	——
4. Promise breaking	——	——
5. Exploding, shouting	——	——
6. Silence, withdrawal, retreating tears	——	——
7. Abusive speech	——	——
8. Gossip	——	——
9. Complaining, grumbling	——	——
10. Quarrelsome speech	——	——
11. Defensive speech, excuse making, blame shifting	——	——
12. Self-centered, boastful speech	——	——
13. Hasty, presumptuous, know-it-all speech	——	——
14. Nitpicking, fault-finding speech	——	——
15. Constant, back-door messages	——	——

COMMUNICATION TEST #2

Rate yourself and your mate on each category. Discuss your ratings and the reasons for them with each other. Seek to improve all ratings of 3 or lower.

1 = Never; 2 = Rarely; 3 = Sometimes; 4 = Frequently; 5 = Regularly

COMMUNICATION PROMPTERS

	YOU	MATE
1. Nonverbal communication regularly (touch, hugs, smiles, etc.)	____	____
2. Shares time daily	____	____
3. Fun time weekly (recreation, common interests, lots of laughs)	____	____
4. Daily dealing with and resolving conflicts	____	____
5. Quick to ask for forgiveness	____	____
6. Genuine concern	____	____
7. Quick to grant forgiveness	____	____
8. Constructive speech	____	____
9. Use of first person pronouns (singular) when dealing with problems and conflicts	____	____
10. Properly timed speech	____	____
11. Truthfulness (honesty, makes sure of facts)	____	____
12. Allows for differences	____	____
13. Careful listening (without interruption, undivided attention, makes sure really understands other person)	____	____
14. Expresses praise, appreciation, compliments, respect	____	____
15. Gives encouragement when discouraged	____	____
16. Expresses interest in others' personal projects, hobbies, etc.	____	____
17. Communicates love in the primary love language of the other person	____	____

RATE YOUR MARRIAGE INVENTORY

Name _____   **Date** _____

This inventory is designed to evaluate how you are doing in your marriage relationship and to spot problem areas so you may work on correcting them. The inventory will be most beneficial if you will each take it individually and then sit down and discuss your respective answers to each question. Seek to understand clearly your mate's reasons behind the rating. If your ratings pinpoint some difficulties, focus on how to resolve problems. Don't just attack or blame your mate. It will be of no benefit for you to defend yourself. Remember, God does have a solution to every problem if you will only handle your problems and seek to solve them in a Biblical way. View and use this inventory in a constructive way.

Rating scale: Always = 4; Often/frequently = 3; Sometimes = 2; Seldom = 1; Never = 0. Write the number that describes what you judge to be true of your marriage in the blank following each question.

1. Does the fact that Jesus Christ is Lord manifest itself in practical ways in your marriage? _____

2. Do you use the Bible to determine your convictions, decisions and practices in life in general and marriage in particular? _____

3. Do you and your spouse study the Bible and pray together? _____

4. Do you worship God together with other believers? _____

5. Do you serve God together in activities that will build up the church and honor Christ? _____

6. Do you and your spouse seek to please one another? _____

7. Do you ask for forgiveness when you have done something wrong? _____

8. Do you take full responsibility for your thoughts, actions and reactions? _____

9. Do you allow your mate to disagree with you without becoming nasty or punishing? _____

10. Do you allow your spouse to make mistakes without becoming nasty or punishing? _____

11. Do you focus on the things that are commendable, praiseworthy and good about your mate? _____

12. Do you express appreciation to your mate in tangible ways? Do you express gratitude and thanks? _____

13. Do you communicate in an in-depth way with each other daily? _____

14. Do you express your opinions, ideas, plans, aspirations, fears, feelings, likes, dislikes, views, problems, joys, frustrations and annoyances to each other? _____

15. Do you and your mate understand each other when you try to express yourselves? _____

16. Do you do many different things together and enjoy being with each other? Are you involved in common projects? _____

17. Do you show love in many practical and tangible ways? _____

18. Do you still court one another by occasional gifts, unexpected attention, etc.? _____

19. Is your conversation pleasant and friendly? _____

20. Do you pray for one another, support and seek to encourge one another? _____

21. Can you discuss differing viewpoints on values, priorities, religious convictions, politics, etc., without becoming irritated? _____

22. Do you anticipate sexual relations with your partner? _____

23. Are your sexual desires compatible? _____

24. Do you freely discuss your sexual desires with your mate? _____

25. Do you agree about the way money should be spent? _____

26. Do you think your spouse is concerned about your view of how money should be spent? _____

27. Do you agree on how to bring up children? _____

28. Do you refuse to lie to your spouse; are you building your relationship on speaking the truth? Can your spouse put full confidence in whatever you say, knowing that you really mean what you say? _____

29. Do you have a good relationship with your in-laws? Do you appreciate them? _____

30. Do you really respect your spouse? _____

31. Are you glad to introduce your spouse to friends and associates? _____

32. Do you control yourself when you are moody so that you do not disrupt your relationship and inflict your moodiness on others? _____

33. Do you seek to change habits of yours that may cause your spouse discomfort or displeasure? _____

34. Do you make your relationship with your spouse a priority matter? _____

35. Do you treat your mate with respect and dignity? _____

36. Do you accept corrective criticisms graciously? _____

37. Do you agree concerning the roles and responsibilities of husband and wife? _____

38. Are you willing to face, discuss and look for Scriptural solutions to problems without blowing up or attacking the other person or dissolving into tears? _____

39. Do you maintain your own spiritual life through Bible reading, prayer, regular church attendance and fellowship with God's people. _____

TOTAL: _____

*Put a circle around the number of previous items that give you concern about your relationship.

PERSONAL INVENTORY #1

Rate **yourself** on each of the following traits. After each word, put the number from the rating scale which most accurately describes you.

Rating Scale:
1 = Never; 2 = Rarely; 3 = Sometimes; 4 = Frequently; 5 = Regularly

Loving	_____	Patient	_____
Honest	_____	Considerate	_____
Sensitive	_____	Persistent	_____
Good parent	_____	Punctual	_____
Work hard	_____	Disciplined	_____
Keep your word	_____	Sincere	_____
Dependable	_____	Courteous	_____
Doesn't take advantage	_____	Creative	_____
Doesn't use people	_____	Decisive	_____
Not an opportunist	_____	Efficient	_____
Plans ahead	_____	Flexible	_____
Know where you are going	_____	Forgiving	_____
Fair	_____	Generous	_____
Consistent	_____	Frugal	_____
Persevering	_____	Appreciative	_____
Admit wrong	_____	Hospitable	_____
Teachable	_____	Diligent	_____
Analytical	_____	Discerning	_____
Compassionate	_____	Enthusiastic	_____
Cooperative	_____	Courageous	_____
Neat	_____	Conscientious	_____
Objective	_____		

Draw a circle around any rating that causes some problems in your marital relationship.

PERSONAL INVENTORY #2

Rate **your mate** on each of the following traits. After each word, put the number from the rating scale which most accurately describes him/her.

Rating Scale:
1 = Never; 2 = Rarely; 3 = Sometimes; 4 = Frequently; 5 = Regularly

Trait	Rating	Trait	Rating
Loving	_____	Patient	_____
Honest	_____	Considerate	_____
Sensitive	_____	Persistent	_____
Good parent	_____	Punctual	_____
Work hard	_____	Disciplined	_____
Keeps his/her word	_____	Sincere	_____
Dependable	_____	Courteous	_____
Doesn't take advantage	_____	Creative	_____
Doesn't use people	_____	Decisive	_____
Not an opportunist	_____	Efficient	_____
Plans ahead	_____	Flexible	_____
Knows where he/she is going	_____	Forgiving	_____
Fair	_____	Generous	_____
Consistent	_____	Frugal	_____
Persevering	_____	Appreciative	_____
Admit wrong	_____	Hospitable	_____
Teachable	_____	Diligent	_____
Analytical	_____	Discerning	_____
Compassionate	_____	Enthusiastic	_____
Cooperative	_____	Courageous	_____
Neat	_____	Conscientious	_____
Objective	_____		

Draw a circle around any rating that causes some problems in your marital relationship.

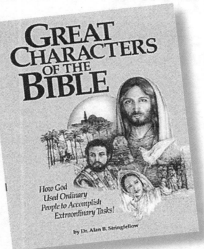
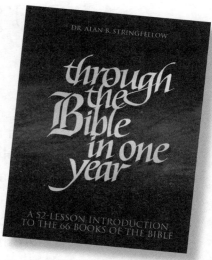